ICARUS ECONOMICS

Also by John Rapley

Why Empires Fall: Rome, America and the Future of the West *(with Peter Heather)*

Twilight of the Money Gods: Economics as Religion

ICARUS ECONOMICS

Why Rich Economies Are Struggling
- and How to Fix Them

John Rapley

Atlantic Books
London

First published in trade paperback in Great Britain in 2026 by
Atlantic Books, an imprint of Atlantic Books Ltd.

Copyright © John Rapley, 2026

The moral right of John Rapley to be identified as the author of this work has been asserted by him in accordance with the Copyright, Designs and Patents Act of 1988.

All rights reserved. No part of this publication may be reproduced, stored in a retrieval system, or transmitted in any form or by any means, electronic, mechanical, photocopying, recording, or otherwise, without the prior permission of both the copyright owner and the above publisher of this book.

No part of this book may be used in any manner in the learning, training or development of generative artificial intelligence technologies (including but not limited to machine learning models and large language models (LLMs)), whether by data scraping, data mining or use in any way to create or form a part of data sets or in any other way.

Every effort has been made to trace or contact all copyright holders. The publishers will be pleased to make good any omissions or rectify any mistakes brought to their attention at the earliest opportunity.

10 9 8 7 6 5 4 3 2 1

A CIP catalogue record for this book is available from the British Library.

Trade Paperback ISBN: 978 1 80546 531 7
E-book ISBN: 978 1 80546 532 4

Printed and bound by CPI Group (UK) Ltd, Croydon CR0 4YY

Atlantic Books
An imprint of Atlantic Books Ltd
Ormond House
26–27 Boswell Street
London
WC1N 3JZ

www.atlantic-books.co.uk

Product safety EU representative: Authorised Rep Compliance Ltd., Ground Floor, 71 Lower Baggot Street, Dublin, D02 P593, Ireland. www.arccompliance.com

CONTENTS

Introduction — 1

1 The Story of Our Ascent — 14
2 Transcending Nature's Limits — 40
3 The Pandemic Paradox — 68
4 The Wealth Paradox — 94
5 The Wealth Trap — 123
6 The Kill Switch Within — 147
7 The Icarus Economy — 174
8 The Middle Course — 204
Conclusion — 227

Notes — 238
Index — 255

INTRODUCTION

Man plans, God laughs.
At one time or another, we've all experienced the cold wisdom about hubris in that old Yiddish proverb. For me, it happened one day in 2020.

After spending the Christmas season in Canada visiting my family, I'd flown back to London to pack up my flat, say goodbye to old friends, go back to Cambridge one last time and prepare for my imminent onward journey to Johannesburg. Having spent the last few years at the university, lecturing in development studies and enjoying college life, with its formal dinners and lunchtime fellowship, I'd started to feel a yearning to return to the global frontier.

But no sooner had I landed in London for what was only ever intended to be a short layover than God laughed at us humans on an epic scale. Here we'd all been, making not just plans for dream vacations or elaborate weddings or new lives on the southern tip of Africa, but indeed making God-like plans to build utopias from endless economic growth, colonize the moon and create a superhuman race by blending technology into ourselves, when nature came along and shut it all down with a microscopic bug, one so powerful it brought the world economy to a halt and forced us to cower in our homes.

With the borders closed everywhere, I was stranded. Hoping, as everyone did, that this disruption would last only a matter of weeks, I turned my attention to the manuscript of a book I was writing. But with the publishing industry shutting down until further notice, it soon became apparent that the book would not be published the following year, as planned. Meanwhile, the weeks became months, and I found myself sinking into my thoughts and reflecting on the state of the world, trying to make sense of what had happened to me. To all of us.

There were lots of memes then circulating on social media about the forced retreat of human activity leaving nature free to heal itself, as birdsong erupted and animals roamed our streets, while we sheltered indoors and watched from our windows. However, this felt different. It felt more like nature taking revenge. As if it had a kill switch, one that was triggered whenever we moved too fast in our efforts to transform our world, or imagined ourselves to be gods rather than just another species on this planet. My mind went back to James Lovelock's controversial 'Gaia hypothesis', which conceived the earth as a huge, complex, living organism with feedback loops that regulated the conditions needed to sustain life and which, like any host organism, could engineer hostile conditions to expel unwanted intruders. Seen through this lens, our disregard for nature prior to its angry response would have amounted to the pride that went before a fall.

The idea of a harsh and angry nature wasn't entirely new to me. Having lived so much of my life in the Global South, I'd come to see how narratives of nature as a nurturing, gentle mother only made sense in the context of places that had already fully tamed it. For most of human history, indeed for most of humanity today, the relationship of humans to nature has remained one laced with struggle, in which nature can alternately be friend or foe – the giver or withholder of rain, of health or indeed of wealth. Nevertheless, I'd grown up in that small sliver of the globe that had broken free from nature, the West,[1] where the story had become one of dramatic triumph, as humans confronted the challenges nature posed, overcame them, and in the process improved themselves. Like everyone in the West, I'd been raised to believe that we were merely further along in this story than our fellow citizens in the developing world, but that if they ever caught up to us they would come to live this tale as we did.

Because this narrative of progress presumed the present to be inherently better than the past, since we had progressed further than our ancestors, I called it the modern tale – from the Latin *modo*, meaning the present moment. In this tale's narrative arc, underpinning our progress and driving it forward was our transformation of our natural environment so as to make it more productive: the discovery of new ways to raise farm output, the invention of machines that could turn fossilized matter into energy, legal innovations that nudged producers to become more efficient and ambitious, medical advances that uncovered the role of germs and pollution in illness and enabled huge prolongations of human life.

All these developments made our societies healthier and richer. Starting around the time Columbus landed in the Americas, following millennia of stagnant incomes, human productivity began a slow but steady ascent, rising from about $1,300 global per capita income (in today's money) to $1,500 at the start of the nineteenth century.[2] And then, things went into overdrive. Over the next two centuries, global per capita income rose another twelve times over in real terms, making possible all manner of improvements to conditions of existence. Huge improvements that changed human life beyond recognition: a mother's death in childbirth went from being ubiquitous to a rare tragedy,[3] infant mortality plunged – whereas for most of human history, one in two children didn't make it to adulthood,[4] today fewer than one in twenty-five suffer that fate – and countless diseases were all but banished by better sanitation, healthcare and medicines. Nature literally lost the ability to put the brakes on humanity's soaring ambitions, as we discovered first air then space travel, and found ways to transport ourselves across the world virtually and instantaneously using digital technologies.

Not only did this transformed world reflect our evolution, but it also enabled humans to free themselves from the bondage of nature, to find new ways to tame and exploit it. Whereas our very earliest ancestors led a most precarious existence, living at the mercy of the elements and the wildlife that preyed upon them, humans had gained the upper hand in the conflict with nature. They bounced back from natural disasters, resuming daily life, gradually moving on to higher planes of existence as they emerged, stronger, more resilient and wiser than before. Even the worst disasters nature threw at us couldn't thwart this evolution.

On the face of it, therefore, the lesson for our time was clear. Confronted with the first truly global pandemic in the form of Covid-19, history showed that if a natural disaster on a scale of the medieval Black Death, which had wiped out a third of Europe's population, couldn't halt the advance of humanity, nothing would. And so it came to pass. Thanks to modern medicine, scientific advancement and the genius of modern bureaucracy, governments responded rapidly to the coronavirus pandemic and in very short order brought the situation under control. Whereas the plagues of antiquity left bodies to pile up in the streets, this one killed a comparatively infinitesimal fraction of a per cent of humanity. Within a couple of years, we had moved on.

Well before then, in anticipation of the end of the pandemic, a new narrative had begun to emerge among economists. Not only could nature not thwart our progress, they said, but we'd bounce back from this pandemic even better and stronger and, above all, richer than before. As soon as economies reopened, a massive backlog of pent-up spending would be unleashed that would create a self-sustaining cycle of powerful growth. The *Financial Times* opened 2021 saying, 'Hello Roaring Twenties'.[5] *The Economist* echoed the optimism, saying the pandemic had accelerated the adoption of technology,[6] with McKinsey estimating a consequent doubling of productivity growth.[7] And sure enough when the lockdowns were lifted and we returned to our offices, we filled the restaurants and shopping centres and packed international flights as we worked through the backlog of spending we'd planned prior to what, by the standards of history, turned out to be a brief interruption. Quicker than ever, normal life resumed.

Except, it didn't. Not like before, at any rate. For my part, I was surprised anyone thought it would. I could foresee, given the unusual vantage point I'd acquired from years of living on the frontier between the developed and developing worlds – growing up in one, moving to the other, then going back and forth regularly between the two – how such an event would change the world forever. I'd already observed how economic development itself changed people and their societies, and how their reaction to adversity could vary in consequence. We were not the 'representative agents' of neoclassical economic theory who would respond similarly to similar stimuli, but had ourselves evolved in differing ways that would greatly vary our responses to the shock.

So on 1 January 2021, I published an essay in a Canadian newspaper making exactly this point: that there would not be a Roaring Twenties, any rebound would be short-lived, and the West would decline relative to the rising periphery, that is, the developing economies, many of which had once been European colonies or subject to European empires.[8] And in fact the world into which we emerged after the pandemic turned out to be quite different from the one we left behind. The progress we long took for granted was slowing rapidly. Most notably, the economic advancement that had run through the history of humanity's ascent, and that sustained and accompanied all our rebounds from previous natural disasters, was waning. Whereas back in the 1960s, annual growth in global per capita gross domestic product (GDP) averaged around 3 per cent, in the decades since it never even reached 2 per cent. Since the end of the pandemic, it fell closer to 1 per cent.

Today, the picture becomes even more revealing when you break global growth into its geographic components. Most poor countries bounced back from the pandemic fairly quickly, and some of them resumed growing at rapid rates. But the world's richest economies, after sharp but brief recoveries from their lockdowns, largely slowed to a crawl. In per capita terms, some, like Canada, even started going backwards – which is to say, their citizens started getting poorer. Even the US, whose continued robust growth elicited talk of American exceptionalism, kept growing mainly by running up huge debts to keep Americans in the living standards to which they'd grown accustomed. Once the patience of creditors wore thin and they began demanding higher interest rates on the money they loaned the country, which began happening in 2025, the US economy also began to slow down.

While writing my book at the time, *Why Empires Fall*, I knew that the pandemic hadn't started this slowdown; it had in fact begun years earlier. But as I compiled the notes for my new book and began experimenting with various economic models, I kept returning to this idea that nature might have a sort of kill switch after all, Covid-19 being an instance of it. Most tellingly, what the pandemic revealed was the unusual way this kill switch affected the economies of the West, something that predictions of a Roaring Twenties had missed. In a complete inversion of the modern tale with which I'd grown up, those countries that had advanced the furthest and appeared to have most completely triumphed over nature were often taking the hardest knocks – because there was growing evidence that their slowdowns and reversals were not cyclical but structural, and would therefore endure, while developing economies would continue growing. I was struck then with the analogy to the ancient tale of Icarus – that eventually, you could rise so high that you lost your wings, whereupon you began falling back towards earth.

But most intriguing of all was that the brakes which nature appeared to be placing on further economic progress – the impediments to further growth or the added expenses that ate into what growth there was – weren't located primarily in the outside world, which is to say our natural environment. Covid-19 was only the latest in a string of zoonotic pandemics that have increased in frequency and virulence since the late twentieth century, to which we can now add the multifarious effects of climate change, including extreme weather and the consequent worsening of floods and wildfires, the growing strains on infrastructure and electricity grids due to rising temperatures, crop failures and the inflation of insurance costs, and many other growth-constraining environmental feedback loops that we'll go on to examine. These are well documented, and their rising economic toll, from the rapidly increasing price tag of damage to property and infrastructure from extreme weather (over $300 billion globally each year and growing quickly[9]) to the rising cost of food production[10] due to the effects of climate change (which drive up interest rates and thus further slow growth) are starting to receive serious attention from economists and the industries in the forefront of absorbing them, such as insurance and construction.

Yet if these exogenous shocks were in fact the principal form that natural feedback loops took, we'd still expect the countries that have done the least harm to the natural environment, namely the poorest countries, to bear the greatest toll, simply because they lack the resources to safeguard against such shocks or to rebuild when they suffer hits from them. That is, in fact, what most of the literature on the economic effects of climate change presumes – that climate injustice must be added to a long string of other injustices that resulted from the rise of the developed world at the expense of the former periphery.

But that doesn't seem to be what's happening. As we shall learn in this book, richer countries may actually be taking bigger economic hits than poor ones from the damaging effects of these feedback loops. Although they have far more resources with which to respond to natural shocks, and indeed are deploying them aggressively, it isn't helping them to bounce back more quickly. On the contrary, each shock seems to slow them more. That appears to be because the biggest change that results from this apparent paradox of progress – that the richer we get, the harder it becomes to stay rich – is the change that has occurred within each of us.

This is the bold and novel argument that this book will make: that this Icarus effect operates not merely in the world around us, but even more importantly within each and every one of us. It will show that economic growth triggers a cycle of behavioural and social changes whose effect, when aggregated, is to progressively inhibit a society's economic dynamism while imposing new costs on that society, with the strength of these effects rising as a country grows richer. Meanwhile, the accumulation of wealth creates demands for its preservation that increasingly weigh on growth, to the point that they ultimately erode a society's stock of wealth.

Wealth changes both individuals and their societies in a manner that can be likened to ageing – slowing them down, making them less resilient, and inhibiting their agility and flexibility. In addition, wealth literally ages a society, raising the average age of the population, which in turn alters its spending and investment decisions in ways that slow and even block growth, leading a society to prioritize wealth preservation over (riskier) wealth creation. Not only does a large stock of wealth slow a society's economic growth but it also makes it more vulnerable to the exogenous shocks that result from environmental change – both because it has a greater stock of wealth to protect, and because its natural ability to bounce back from shocks diminishes. Since the natural resilience of a country thus diminishes as its wealth rises, contending with exogenous shocks requires a greater outlay of resources: the richer a country is, the harder it falls, and so the more it must spend to cushion and recover from that fall.

This is the point that some Western countries have now reached. It has become so expensive for them to stay rich that they are actually eroding their stock of wealth and eating into their future income, the result being a declining standard of living. This is how nature's kill switch operates, by both triggering exogenous shocks from environmental feedback loops and then weakening our ability to withstand and overcome them. The end result is an apparent paradox: growth ultimately ends in degrowth, not because humans choose it but because, it would seem, it chooses them. Rather as the public their agility and flexibility. In addition, wealth literally ages a society, raising the average age of the population, which in turn alters its spending and investment decisions in ways that slow and even block growth, leading a society to prioritize wealth preservation over (riskier) wealth creation. Not only does a large stock of wealth slow a society's economic growth but it also makes it more vulnerable to the exogenous shocks that result from environmental change – both because it has a greater stock of wealth to protect, and because its natural ability to bounce back from shocks diminishes. Since the natural resilience of a country thus diminishes as its wealth rises, contending with exogenous shocks requires a greater outlay of resources: the richer a country is, the harder it falls, and so the more it must spend to cushion and recover from that fall.

This is the point that some Western countries have now reached. It has become so expensive for them to stay rich that they are actually eroding their stock of wealth and eating into their future income, the result being a declining standard of living. This is how nature's kill switch operates, by both triggering exogenous shocks from environmental feedback loops and then weakening our ability to withstand and overcome them. The end result is an apparent paradox: growth ultimately ends in degrowth, not because humans choose it but because, it would seem, it chooses them. Rather as the public health literature has found that autoimmune diseases seem most prevalent in the societies that have gone the furthest towards eradicating disease, it would appear that a society can grow so rich it eventually begins to eat its own wealth (and possibly even for a similar reason: that the price of comfort may be a loss of resilience and adaptability).

Whether this is inevitable or a function of choices that can be changed remains to be seen. We are in only the very early stages of this transition to degrowth. But what is significant for the purposes of this argument is that when we talk about nature's kill switch, it would appear that what matters most is not the nature around us that we're said to be destroying, but that within us. Our human nature.

All of this may seem bold and radical. In fact, the idea is ancient. Our ancestors warned us this might happen, in stories they told long ago.

1

THE STORY OF OUR ASCENT

It's getting ever harder to deny the reality of climate change. Its effects are becoming inescapable. The weather is stranger, harsher and more unpredictable with longer and hotter heatwaves, periods of heavy rain and flooding followed by droughts, and other forms of 'climate whiplash'. Faced with this new reality, and the prospect of these effects only deepening, how do we respond – do we change our lifestyles, blame someone else and ignore it, trust in some technological bullet to come along and reverse the damage we've done, or just give up and begin planning to colonize new planets, so that in the event of a climate catastrophe on earth, we might start over somewhere else?

Few of us, when faced with such existential questions, spend much time consulting the literature of opposing camps. Even academic economists seldom read much of the literature on how to deal with climate change before taking their stand on the topic. Even if this is your first foray into the subject, you probably already have some answers to the questions posed in the opening paragraph, because all of us fall back on what behavioural economists call heuristics, shortcuts that point us to quick answers to profound questions. And those heuristics come from the stories on which we base our lives.

Stories shape us. We grow up with tales that help us to explain the mysteries of our world – why we are here, where we're going, what's right and what's wrong, what defines success and how to attain it, why we are rich or poor or healthy or sick or loved or lonely. And at the moment, two stories dominate the public discussion of climate change. One depicts economic growth as the hero of the saga, the other makes it the villain. Those who see the economic growth of the last few centuries as the greatest human achievement of all time – and that would include most mainstream economists – point to the progress that has resulted for all humanity: we've gone from a world in which famine was a regular feature of life to one that produces more than enough food to feed all the planet's human inhabitants,[1] where modern medicine has doubled lifespans, and where working-class shoppers have access to a lifestyle that even medieval aristocrats could only have dreamed of. Given the track record of growth, therefore, the pro-growth school of thought is confident that the climate crisis will be solved by new technologies that reduce or neutralize carbon emissions, and that new technologies arise from economic growth – ergo more growth, cleaner world. For instance, as economic growth consumes more resources, those resources become more scarce and thus more expensive, prompting innovations that use the resources more efficiently, ultimately curtailing demand for them.

The anti-growth or degrowth school takes the opposite view. While its proponents acknowledge that innovations *could* enable the world to do more with less, they note that in practice it hasn't worked out that way: the richer the world gets, the more carbon emissions it produces, putting us on a treadmill towards doom. And since most of the carbon emissions causing climate change have been emitted since the start of the Industrial Revolution, and particularly since the middle of the last century, excessive growth is undeniably the villain of this drama, and even the heroic exploits attributed to it by its proponents are its own doing. For instance, while growth has given us the means to banish hunger, we haven't done so, since nearly a billion people daily go without food for a day or more at a time.[2] Social historians have long argued that even the social progress of the industrial age resulted less from the natural machinations of growth as from working-class struggles to secure their share of a growing pie – that left to its own devices, growth would have bypassed most humans.

The growth/degrowth polarity in our discussion of the response to climate change isn't accidental. Both schools emerged in the final decades of the twentieth century as responses to the most extraordinary development in human history – the economic growth of the modern age. This is the starting point for all of the stories we tell of how we got to be where we are today. A few centuries ago, starting in Western Europe and then spreading outwards through the empires it was able to seize on the back of its newly acquired power, an economic system we call capitalism raised the output of human beings. Agronomists found new ways of increasing farm output, engineers developed better agricultural implements or machines to raise labour productivity, medics and scientists discovered the causes and cures of disease, and entrepreneurs found ways to use this new knowledge to inject dynamism into hitherto stationary economies.

At the dawn of this new age, the average human lived on the equivalent of what in today's money would be about $1,000 a year.[3] Today, the average human lives off more than fifteen times that – the richest humans, countless times more. This extraordinary rise in incomes was then translated into improvements in well-being that would have seemed inconceivable to our ancestors. Life prior to the modern period really could be nasty, brutish and short: brigands ruled the countryside and the cities were unsafe, the water unsanitary, the food inadequate. To sustain life, we need to consume somewhere in the vicinity of 2,000 calories of food energy each day, but in the seventeenth century the average person got barely that, which meant that in years of bad harvest they starved. But thereafter, as farming techniques improved, those averages rose until today we have all but banished natural starvation from the globe (the persistent problem of global hunger that remains resulting from inequality and poor policy).

Just why this economic revolution broke out when and where it did – in Western Europe in the second half of the second millennium – remains a mystery, since the region was then something of a backwater, well behind the industrial powerhouses of India and China. Its sudden leap forward, in a very short period of time, appeared to come from nowhere and so stirs considerable scholarly debate. Culture and religion seem to have played a part, as did warfare, geography and the natural environment, and possibly a good admixture of plain luck. But its ultimate progeny was an Industrial Revolution that would change our world forever, including the way we conceived of ourselves and our relationship to nature.

After millennia of stagnation, the world economy began growing, and growing fast. In a short space of time, the human species went from being poor to being rich; from living at nature's mercy to bending it to its will. This complete inversion of what was seen as the natural state of being required a radical rethink about what it meant to be human, and indeed why we were here on this planet.

How we rose above nature, and changed our own nature

For our ancestors, nature had been capricious. If the rains didn't come, or if they came too much, or if the herds didn't return, people would starve. Various other natural disasters could befall them at any moment, and death in childbirth was a routine part of life. Thus, the myths that emerged from these conditions of existence tended to show nature as volatile, unpredictable and harsh in its judgements, presenting humans as subject to laws that lay beyond our control – laws that, if we violated them, would result in some kind of supernatural punishment. From the vantage point of most humans who ever lived, Earth seemed at best a reluctant host, behaving as if it only grudgingly tolerated our presence, throwing an endless series of natural disasters our way, including diseases, ice ages, mass extinctions, or withholding the rains long enough for people to starve. Our earliest ancestors learned to propitiate jealous or angry gods, or to pray to the animals to succumb to their arrows, just to be able to eat, or for their children to survive.

In consequence, a recurring theme in the myths of antiquity were stories about the dangers of arrogance, or what the Greeks called hubris. From the arrogance of Indra, who thought he could defy moral conventions without consequences in Hindu mythology, or the reason for the opossum's bare tail, as explained in the stories of the Cherokee people, arrogance towards the divine realm would not be tolerated by the gods. Greek myths and epics were filled with heroes who were struck down when they tried to approach or challenge the gods. Babylonian and Canaanite legends held that the planet Venus was a god cast out from Heaven for attempting to occupy the throne of a higher god. Jewish stories carried this forward and ultimately evolved, via Christianity, into the tale of a fallen angel, usually the Devil, cast out of Heaven for thinking he could play the role of God.

Related to this, and present in the 'animistic' elements of religious traditions around the world – many of which evolved into today's great religions – was the belief that nature, being a divine creation, had to be treated with respect and even reverence. Over time, therefore, caution about our place in the world came to be embedded in our cultural heritage, enshrined in moral codes that advised us to know our place in the divine realm and to live in harmony with nature or in accordance with its laws, lest nature takes its revenge. The myths of diverse cultures were filled with tales of the ways in which nature would wreak havoc on humans who disregarded its sovereignty, sending divine chastisement or purges in the forms of plagues, floods or other natural disasters. In the Chinese Confucian tradition, such events were taken as signs that the ruler had lost the 'Mandate of Heaven' and thus become illegitimate, a moral that found a parallel in the Zoroastrian legend of the king Jamshid, who took credit for all his great achievements and saw himself as the lord of nature, his pride leading to the ruin of his kingdom.[4]

However, this idea, of a sort of kill switch in nature triggered by human hubris, lost its salience amid the economic transformation of the last two centuries. After millennia of living at the mercy of nature, humans now found themselves its masters. The old myths could explain none of this dramatic turnaround, so we began crafting new stories. A common thread in these stories was that we'd discovered science and reason and thereby succeeded in turning nature from a reluctant host into a bountiful servant, using nature's resources to transform our lives and the world in which we lived.

In the late nineteenth century, this modern

mythology gave rise to what would be called the conflict thesis. The American academic John William Draper opened his 1875 book *History of the Conflict between Religion and Science* by saying 'The history of Science… is a narrative of the conflict of two contending powers, the expansive force of the human intellect on one side, and the compression arising from traditionary faith and human interests on the other.'[5] Draper had attended the famous 1860 Oxford debate about evolution between the Anglican archbishop Samuel Wilberforce and the agnostic 'social Darwinian' T.H. Huxley in which, challenged ironically by Wilberforce whether it was from his grandmother's or grandfather's side he had descended from apes, Huxley had replied he'd rather be descended from apes than from an obscurantist like Wilberforce. In the dramatic arc of the tale Draper now told by distilling the histories of the Enlightenment and the scientific and industrial revolutions into one seamless narrative, humans had been held back for millennia by religion, tradition and superstition. Spiritual death, though, had brought them material birth: after the dramatic clash between science and faith that ran through the early modern period, the triumph of reason over religion freed humans to become godlike in their creativity. Rejecting the authority of tradition, satisfied that the present was always better than the past and that the future would be better yet, this new mythology celebrated youth and novelty over age and authority.

Especially in those countries in the vanguard of the Industrial Revolution, this narrative found a ready audience. In 1851, Britain staged the Great Exhibition, building a futuristic cathedral entirely of glass and steel in London's Hyde Park, called the Crystal Palace. Inviting the nations of the world to showcase their wares, the exhibition provided the country with an opportunity to mark the achievement of its Industrial Revolution and the greatness of its empire. Everyone who was anyone in British society attended, including Charles Dickens, who took time from his writing schedule to visit the exhibition. With poet and journalist Richard Horne, Dickens would then co-author a report that embodied this emerging myth.

In it, they wrote of 'the revolving, dioptric, and catadioptric apparatus of lighthouses; models of railways, of iron bridges, of self-supporting suspension-bridges, of submarine steam-propellers, of the great tubular bridge', and of the proposed 'grand ship canal through the Isthmus of Suez', and adjudged that 'we are moving in a right direction towards some superior condition of society – politically, morally, intellectually, and religiously'.[6] Even if it was clear to them that Britain led the world in this advance, Dickens and Horne left no doubt that this brighter future was accessible to all nations. Those who chose to resist progress – they singled out

China – would be overwhelmed by the resulting higher civilizations. They mockingly depicted an Orient that had decided to cling to past glories and thus had no future:

> In China, there are the Great Wall, and the Imperial Palace at Pekin, and the pagodas with their turned-up corners and their bells, and the temple and bridges, and the various teapot works, with few additions, if any, and probably none, all just as they were centuries ago, suggesting the idea of the same Emperor having sat upon the same enamelled porcelain throne during the whole time, with the same thin-arched pair of elevated eyebrows, admiring and wondering, with the same inanity, at the same inanimate perfection of himself and all around him.

They concluded that given the choice between clinging to tradition and moving into the modern age, only 'an odd, barbarous, or eccentric nation' like China would choose to keep past ways.

This modern tale was not one of nature's sovereignty over all species on earth, but of human triumph over nature and all its other species. As science and reason took precedence over superstition, myth and religion in shaping our approach to the world, humans emancipated themselves from nature and the tyranny of spiritual guides. Like an unbound Prometheus, we then began to soar to hitherto unimaginable heights. Economic growth took off. We conquered the oceans, launched ourselves into space, built skyscrapers that towered into thin air, went far towards ending hunger and discovered cures for most of the diseases that had ravaged our progenitors. And today, as scientists raise the possibility of eternal human life, we contemplate the possibility not merely of displacing the gods, but of becoming gods, with visions of a 'singularity' in which advanced technology is inserted into human bodies to create a new race of superhuman, ultra-intelligent beings.

Whereas our ancestors created myths and stories of Promised Lands, golden ages and Gardens of Eden to give them strength in their daily struggles, we brought their dreams to life in the here and now. We went from living at the edge of survival, eking out an existence that put us just above the state of animals, to being the richest, strongest, healthiest and safest beings ever to have walked this planet. It went without saying that in this new story of humanity's place in the world, hubris ceased to be a curse: after all, freeing ourselves from fear of excessive pride is what made it possible for us to transcend nature's limits.

The moral of this modern tale was that humans could scale any height and solve any problem if they freed themselves from old qualms and applied their ingenuity.

The birth of a new science of progress

Not everyone embraced this modern tale, though. From the dawn of the industrial age, many artists and intellectuals rejected the science and rationality of this story of progress to focus on what humans were losing to growth – their spiritual sides, their sense of the sublime and of an enchanted realm that lay beyond the access of human rationality, reached only through mysticism or art or poetry. These Romantics, as they came to be known, saw humans as spiritual and not merely physical creatures, beings who thus became degraded and dissatisfied when they drowned in a swamp of purely physical, material satisfactions, which in turn could damage the natural ecosystems upon which they depended for their lives. Romanticism would provide much of the inspiration for the modern rebellion against industrial, consumer society, from the hippies to the early ecology movement, which felt that human distance from nature was degrading the many while enriching the few. It would also provide an intellectual foundation for what would later become known as the degrowth movement.

The advocates of degrowth, however, would go beyond a purely aesthetic critique of growth to point to its many material failings. Jason Hickel, who has engaged in running arguments with mainstream economists, shows that using growth as a metric for human welfare produces many absurdities. For example, national accounts regard a pound sterling's worth of tear gas as equivalent to a pound sterling's worth of healthcare; the price of both is determined not by any moral norm but by the market (which is dominated by very rich consumers who may, or may not, have any interest in creating a just society).[7] Timothée Parrique similarly points out that even though it wouldn't result in any decline in human well-being and would actually improve sustainability, eliminating wasteful output like planned obsolescence and advertising would nevertheless show up as an economic contraction.[8] Kate Raworth, who while not a degrowth economist is sometimes lumped among them by her critics because of her focus on sustainability, uses the analogy of human development to critique what she sees as the idealization of growth by mainstream economics: although humans finish their physical growth in late adolescence, their development continues long afterwards.[9] Thus, the economic growth we have achieved over the last few centuries has been a boon, but since we now have the resources to solve many of humanity's problems, we should focus on that rather than further growth, since the latter is becoming a threat to the natural environment and therefore to our own future well-being.

We will return to the topic of degrowth later, but within the economics discipline, such views still receive a frosty reception. Branko Milanovic, who being a left-leaning scholar shows how united the broad spectrum of the economics profession is around its modern orthodoxy, criticizes degrowth fiercely, saying that while GDP may be an imperfect metric of progress it is 'fairly accurate overall' since 'income indeed buys you health and happiness'.[10] Instead, mainstream economics, which arose with modernity and first took a clear form in the late nineteenth century, right around the time the conflict thesis emerged, still guides most governments in their approach to climate change.

Although economic thought had featured in the writing and teaching of political thinkers for over two thousand years, economics as we now know it originated in the eighteenth century, when it emerged as a tool of statecraft and a branch of moral philosophy. Though it would subsequently integrate scientific method into its work, it has always remained at heart a moral philosophy, its ultimate aim being to create a good, prosperous society in which humans could flourish. Whereas a pure scientist tries to understand the world as it is, what Marx said of his trade has always been true of economists: their aim is to change the world for the better.

When it came to its moral premises, economics embodied the modern mythology of scientific progress. Although, in its earliest days, thinkers like Adam Smith, David Ricardo and John Stuart Mill assumed that nature would pose limits to economic expansion, and that growth would gradually approach zero, whereupon it settled into a steady state – putatively the reason that the critic Thomas Carlyle called economics the 'dismal science' – in the course of the nineteenth century a new conviction took hold: that technological progress, and the constant churn and consequent renewal of a market economy, would enable economies to grow endlessly. Plotting the way forward required economic thinkers to shed all the prejudices they had inherited from the past so as to focus squarely on the future. The famed Cambridge economist Arthur Pigou argued that such men of science no longer needed to study history, any more than a modern psychiatrist would study phrenology, since all the past could provide them in the way of knowledge were some 'inadequate solutions that were offered centuries ago'.[11] The present, in this view, would necessarily yield more advanced methods than the past.

Around the time most of the world's European colonies gained their independence, the global economy entered an unprecedented and prolonged period of economic growth. As we'll explore in greater depth in the next chapter, in the second half of the twentieth century, humanity's real per capita incomes doubled. In Western countries, they tripled, a rate of growth that had never been seen before. The period from about 1948 through to the first oil shock in 1973, which just happened to overlap with the rise to independence of most of the world's colonies, witnessed the highest growth rate ever. The future for these young states, and for the citizens of the West, then seemed limited only by their imaginations.

These income gains were then channelled into huge, measurable improvements in human well-being. This was the age in which the welfare state as we know it came into full existence, with all Western countries building safety nets of varying generosity in the form of housing, income support, healthcare and unemployment insurance. In developing countries, governments engineered hugely ambitious programmes of modernization by investing in new industries, building new cities, and using trade barriers to protect the local market from imports, thereby nurturing the growth of local manufacturing.

Economists took no small amount of credit for this progress. Western governments had then largely coalesced around an economic model known as the Keynesian synthesis, which blended free markets with state guidance. In developing countries, a similar strain known as structuralism advocated extensive use of state direction and nurturing to develop local industries and accelerate growth. The vision that emerged was of an enlightened, state-led market economy that allowed human ingenuity to seek its rewards. The optimism of the postwar period was heady. Economists believed they had found the keys to economic management that would enable eternal growth and an end to recessions. Nor did they see any reason to expect this would ever change. In particular, they no longer had cause to believe that there were natural limits to growth, because every time a given resource grew scarce from overuse, human ingenuity found ways to locate new ones, extract them more efficiently or switch to substitutes.

In effect, this triumph of humanity over nature was instigated by an inversion of an ancient code. For millennia, the moral tales of humanity had emphasized the need for humility in the face of nature. The modern myth demanded the opposite, that humans take pride in their achievement, since there was nothing that could stop them from advancing ever higher. The twist this tale put on one ancient story of hubris would turn out to be revealing.

In the Greek myth of Icarus, the hero flew too high and, in his determination to reach the sun, ended up crashing to earth as the sun put him back in his place. But in the modern retelling, his descendants not only found a new way to approach the sun but actually managed to seize control of it and the energy it produced.

Long before our ancestors walked the earth, the sun had been storing its energy beneath the planet's surface. Photosynthesis, the natural process by which sunlight gave rise to life, converted energy into plant matter, which then became the basis of all animal food chains, which further stored energy in their bodies. As plants and animals died and sank into the earth's surface, what remained fossilized. And so it went on, from one aeon to the next, until one day humans discovered the secret to releasing this energy from its age-old sleep.

Initially, humans used fire mainly to warm themselves and for cooking, using only recently dead plant life, like wood or peat. But in time, they discovered coal, and later oil and gas, finding ways to ignite them efficiently. They then devised methods, often in combination with water, to convert the thermal energy thereby released into forms of kinetic energy – the energy that would power the engines that would drive the Industrial Revolution and eventually build the modern world. In due course, they would pour that energy into the automobiles, aeroplanes, trains and rockets that would take us much further than Icarus could have imagined. The energy would power the electrical grids that allowed us to create new inventions like refrigerators, air conditioners, radios, televisions and phones, the ovens and food mixers and coffee grinders that would make our kitchens into small factories, the hairdryers and electric razors and the tools we needed for work or hobbies. With this energy we could play video games and watch movies and sit at computers connected to a vast web of servers that opened up whole new worlds to us; we could make our streets safer with night lighting and our theatres and clubs more enjoyable with PA systems. We were just getting started. Now the stars themselves beckoned us to build the spaceships that would take us to distant galaxies. No sun could stop the modern Icarus. The artificer had become master of all, servant to none.

So, when confronted with the climate crisis, mainstream economics regards it as an unintended, admittedly negative but eminently surmountable consequence of growth, since the same ingenuity that produced the growth in the first place can craft new solutions, like new technology or better policies. We don't need to change our hearts and live a different life. We need only apply our minds. It thus follows that more advanced societies – those with richer and more developed economies and more emancipated from nature – will be more able to address the climate crisis.

But does being compelling make the story true or right?

One evening in Johannesburg early in 2023, I went to a book signing by a well-known British author. Russia's invasion of Ukraine was ongoing, and Donald Trump was back on the campaign trail with promises to go after his enemies and abandon America's friends. So when someone in the audience asked the author if this was as dangerous a time as the 1930s, he answered that the risks of a global conflagration were greater than they had ever been in his lifetime. But then he added an interesting caveat: 'Still, this is the greatest time ever to be alive. We are living longer than ever, are healthier and richer than ever, and have more opportunities than our ancestors could have dreamed of.'

The modern tale. After he and I chatted briefly and I left the large crowd to get their books signed, I drove out through the back entrance. Reaching the gate, I turned and saw one of the city's army of recyclers about to cross my path. His face was creased with premature wrinkles, his wiry body straining from the labours of walking the city's streets from before dawn until well after dusk dragging his wheeled pallet laden with the most valuable bits of glass, plastic and tin extracted from people's weekly rubbish and for which, after a day's efforts, he could exchange for the price of a budget meal in one of the neighbourhood's fast-food restaurants. I wondered: how would he respond if I told him that this is the greatest time to be alive, that thanks to human progress he'd be able to do this for ten more years than he otherwise would have?

While the story of progress thanks to science, reason and self-belief may be what explains the dramatic emancipation of humans from the tyranny of nature in the last two centuries, that's not why we believe it. As compelling and plausible as the story sounds, hardly anyone actually approaches it sceptically, treating its claims as hypotheses that require testing and challenge. Rather, for those of us in the West (that part of the world most altered by the Industrial Revolution), the modern tale rings true because it helps us to explain our place in the world – our extraordinarily privileged place, where at its peak at the turn of the millennium we had an average income some sixty times greater than that of a person in the developing world. A narrative that credited our success to our individual effort freed us from any obligations to those less-privileged citizens, who remain the mass of humanity. It would have had a powerful appeal even if it had been entirely untrue.

And it certainly wasn't that. When you do look closely at what made possible the ascent of the West over the rest of the world, it becomes clear that individualism, good institutions and scientific advancement all played their part. It's just that those weren't the only things that did. So too did the surpluses extracted from slavery, the markets and unequal trade terms secured by empire, and a postwar global trading system that for several decades privileged Western countries over the newly independent states of the Global South. The story, in short, is more complicated than the simple triumph of the rational individual.

Moreover, to maintain the plot line of science and reason's victory over ignorance, the modern tale had to portray pre-modern belief systems as less rational than they were. Much of the story of existential struggle between science and religion at the cusp of modernity was based on invented episodes, like the idea that medieval scholars considered the world flat (they didn't), or that the scholars of the scientific revolution spurned faith when in fact they were usually religious men who thought science could draw us closer to God. Perhaps most risible of all was the claim that the old religions produced slavery and the Enlightenment ended it, when in fact Enlightenment thinkers quite easily justified slavery for sustaining economic progress, whereas the abolitionist campaigners were usually motivated by their religious convictions that slavery was evil.

However, origin tales can't accommodate nuance. They need a hero (in this case, the rational individual) and a villain (the traditional, anti-rational church and its web of superstitions), and a dramatic arc of conflict, ascent and triumph. The rest is extraneous and must be stripped out. If what results strays far from the truth, so be it. What makes a story good, what makes a movie or song good, is not that it reveals truth, but that it touches *our* truth – it gives us a narrative that enables us to make sense of our life in a way that is satisfying and meaningful.

Most importantly, it gives us the toolbox with which to approach life's challenges – not least today's 'polycrises' of slowing economies, epidemics, climate change and the refugee flows they are prompting. Because the climate crisis is a global crisis, the solutions will need to be applied globally. So it's necessary to consider whether this story is true not just for us in the West, but for everyone, everywhere. Is scientific progress, to put it simply, all that we've cracked it up to be? Or have we oversimplified a complex tale and thus blinded ourselves to the moral or behavioural changes we must make to ensure we continue to thrive as a species?

The truth is that for much if not most of humanity today, the modern tale can sound rather odd and alien, resembling science fiction more than fact. Whether we believe it or not largely reflects our vantage point. Which leaves us with the ultimate question: but is it true? Could modernity eventually conquer the globe, emancipate all humans from nature and create a wonderful future? That is the position taken by exponents of the modern tale, that its only shortcoming is that progress has yet to reach all corners of the planet but that when it finally does, the hurdles facing my Johannesburg recycler will fall away just as they did in Western societies. Degrowthers retort that if the rest of the world grows to the point where it catches up with the West, the resulting carbon emissions will push climate change so far that our future as a species will come into question. Is the modern tale based on a blind faith in growth, or can we continue to produce the innovations needed to rectify any of the problems caused by growth?

Today, the ecological consequences of the growth of the last two centuries, including climate change, have started throwing up what amount to live experiments in the testing of the modern tale. Humans today confront the threats of pollution, extreme weather, desertification, crop failures, water scarcities and an increase in zoonotic diseases and antibiotic-resistant superbugs, all of which could potentially cause increased conflict, a massive displacement of population and the uncontrolled migrations so feared by Western leaders. Faced with these new challenges, we can see how well the human emancipation from nature has prepared us for the unintended challenges that resulted from growth. Will further growth tip the planet over the edge by accelerating climate change faster than we can adapt to it, giving rise to recurrent crises caused by ecological shocks? Or will further growth yield the new technologies and resources we need to tackle all these problems, such as better seed varieties, new drugs and medical procedures, architecture and infrastructure that can resist more violent weather conditions, better delivery systems, and so on?

As we proceed to look at these challenges in more detail, we'll see that the story begins to take some unusual turns – that while emancipation from nature reduces some of our vulnerabilities, it can also create new ones; and that while progress can mean ascent, it can also apply to a descent. The moral of the tale starts to get a bit more complex than we first thought.

2

TRANSCENDING NATURE'S LIMITS

Building the new Jerusalem

When Europe and Asia emerged from their bunkers at the end of the Second World War, their prospects looked bleak. In Britain, the wartime burst of government spending that had ensured everyone had a job and a meal left a debt overhang that forced severe austerity on the nation. Jobs were cut, wartime rationing continued and the winter of 1946–47, when the country nearly froze to death, left many Britons feeling worse off, their incomes lower than before. Nowhere was immune because even the US, completely sheltered from the war's ravages, experienced a slump immediately after it ended. Things were even worse in Europe, though, where the destruction of whole cities had left millions homeless, destitute and hungry, with no apparent end in sight. In Germany, the American occupation government was even pondering a plan to ensure the country went back to being an agrarian economy so that it would never again be rich enough to fight another war. Progress seemed at an end.

But during that cold winter, Washington was busily hatching a new, very different plan for Europe. As it watched Europe's communist parties ride a wave of election victories with stories of a future utopia, the Americans realized that their future prosperity depended on friendly governments overseeing growing economies, which postwar deprivation was making unlikely. So that summer, Secretary of State George Marshall unveiled a new plan that would pour aid money into Europe's reconstruction while opening America's markets to European factories.

The effects of this 'Marshall Plan' were almost instantaneous. By the following year, a boom had begun, one that would last through a quarter-century of extraordinary growth on a scale that had no precedent in history. It would transform the world beyond anything even people who were adults at its start would have recognized from their childhoods, so rapid was the pace of change. Between 1948 and 1973 – a time known in English as the 'golden age', in French as the 'thirty glorious years', in German simply as 'the miracle' – the planet's economic output more than doubled. In North

America and Western Europe, it tripled. Moreover, thanks in no small part to the strength of the labour movement at the time, the benefits spread far and wide. 'Let us be frank about it,' declared British Prime Minister Harold Macmillan in a 1957 speech, 'most of our people have never had it so good. Go around the country, go to the industrial towns, go to the farms and you will see a state of prosperity such as we have never had in my lifetime – nor indeed in the history of this country.'[1]

In his lyrical memoir of childhood, the American author Bill Bryson similarly opined, 'I can't imagine there has ever been a more gratifying time to be alive than America in the 1950s.'[2] There had never before been, and might never again be, a time of such prosperity and seemingly endless possibility. In 1945, scarcely any household in Europe and North America owned a television. Two decades later, virtually all did. In Europe, the same went for cars and refrigerators while in America the average family went from having one car to two. The list of electric items that went from being novelties to ubiquitous in just a matter of years is dazzling: dishwashers, washing machines, tumble dryers, electric irons, vacuum cleaners, home stereos, lawnmowers, kitchens equipped with mixers, toasters, blenders, and bathroom cupboards filled with electric razors, hairdryers and curling tongs.

And while most of these gains flowed to Western countries, the sheer pace of their economic ascent ensured that almost the entire globe got dragged along too. This happened to be the period in which Europe's remaining great empires – the French, British, Dutch, Belgian and eventually Portuguese – after initially fighting to regain colonies over which they'd lost some hold during the war, were forced to give them up, resulting in an explosion of new states. Eager to catch up to their former colonial rulers, these countries exported their farm products and minerals to a ravenous West and used the proceeds to rapidly 'modernize'[3] their burgeoning cities – building roads, futuristic skyscrapers of concrete and glass, schools and universities and hospitals and national stadiums. Coffee from Brazil, cocoa from Ghana, rubber from Indonesia, tea from Sri Lanka, cotton from India – with the world economy booming in the 1950s, young countries were able to fund the rapid transformation of their economies and societies by selling their primary wares into the thriving Western economies. Their governments thus looked forward to a future as equals in the modern world, forcibly wrenching their peoples away from traditions and old ways if need be.

Throughout the history of capitalism, it seldom occurred to anyone that there might be limits to such growth. Romantic unease over the 'Satanic mills' of which the English poet William Blake spoke accompanied the rise of industrial society, but their anxieties were more aesthetic than environmental. No matter what people drew from the land or mined from its soil, plenty more always appeared; no matter how much smoke their fires and furnaces belched into the atmosphere, the wind blew it away and left them with clean air; no matter how much garbage or sewage they dumped into the river, the current always washed it out into a sea so vast it could swallow it without a trace. If in hindsight this seems like complacency, it wasn't necessarily irrational. If the planet felt crowded, that was only because urbanization packed more people together in cities, yet these occupied only a tiny sliver of the planet. The vast majority of the earth's surface remained empty, so much so that in 1950, the world's entire population could have fitted into an area the size of Texas, giving each family a Texas-sized quarter-acre plot on which to build their home. That left plenty of space on the planet to grow their food, and plenty of forests and sea to soak up their pollution.

Nevertheless, the world had never experienced anything quite like the long period of peace and prosperity that followed the war. This age of abundance produced a growing, nagging worry that there might be something wrong with the endless satisfaction of our appetites. To power all the new devices we were obtaining, energy consumption rocketed, and most of it was driven by gas- or oil-powered turbines, given how cheap petroleum was then. In consequence, in the short span of the quarter-century golden age, humanity produced more carbon emissions than it had in its entire prior history.[4] Put differently, after several millennia, through even the dirty, smoky century of the Industrial Revolution, we produced almost no pollution in comparison to the two-decades-long era of tail-finned cars and package holidays to Spain.

Come the 1960s, popular culture in Western countries was thus growing increasingly sceptical of the postwar consumerist culture. Although most economists saw this abundance as the great achievement of modernity, enabling ever rising standards of living, student revolts on European and American campuses mocked the materialism of their parents' generation, a zeitgeist channelled in films like *The Graduate* and *Harold and Maude*.

Radical politics began to take on a new, critical edge that framed this repudiation in revolutionary terms. Whereas socialist parties had long seen industrial society as the end point of development, the gradual emergence of a post-industrial society, as rich economies shifted from manufacturing to services, heralded a relative decline in the weight of the industrial working class. In its place emerged a new radicalism based on youth and 'post-materialist' values,[5] one that now prioritized issues like individual autonomy, sexual freedom, racial and gender equality, and ecology. In place of the old left's adherence to the Soviet model of industrial development, the new left preferred the Maoist experiment with rural communes then under way in China, and guerrilla movements in Global South countries.

Although this critique of industrial society was still largely aesthetic, a concern with sustainability was beginning to manifest itself. By the late 1960s, environmentalism had consequently gone from being a niche, philosophical concern to entering the public domain, with groups like Greenpeace and Friends of the Earth coming into existence and the launch of Earth Day. In 1971, the recipe book *Diet for a Small Planet*, promoting a diet that would be sustainable in an increasingly resource-constrained planet, became a bestseller. Popular discussion of economics now included concerns about pollution, resource and water shortages, accelerated extinctions and the loss of biodiversity, to say nothing of the general ugliness often associated with endless growth. This sudden awareness worked its way into popular culture, with pop songs celebrating nature and fashions acquiring a rustic, earthy aesthetic. Reflecting what it saw as vulgar consumerism and a cult of endless growth, this new Romanticism found beauty in nature and simplicity, and worried about what the new golden age had done to 'mother nature'. As Joni Mitchell put it in her 1970 hit single 'Big Yellow Taxi', 'they paved paradise and put up a parking lot'.

Gaia's revenge

The popularity of the motherly metaphor to describe nature was revealing, though. Depicting the planet as a bountiful and nurturing parent that required our love and care, this new Romanticism betrayed its fundamentally modern roots. It did not hark back to an ancient discourse, but still saw humans as sovereign. It merely enjoined them to use their immense power to save rather than destroy the planet.

However, reflecting the spirit of a less carefree time, scholars began turning a more dispassionate eye to the environmental impacts of rapid economic growth. What their work revealed was a somewhat darker, decidedly less Romantic narrative.

The ecologists came first, producing studies that tried to determine if there were measurable natural limits to economic expansion and, if so, where they lay. In 1968, Garrett Hardin published a scientific article titled 'The Tragedy of the Commons' that would go on to have enormous influence.[6] Reviving the argument made nearly two centuries earlier by the English economist

Thomas Robert Malthus, Hardin argued that the exponential growth of the human population, in a world of finite resources, would eventually produce an ecological crisis, with the food supply running out.

Soon afterwards, a group of scientists convened a meeting in Rome and commissioned a study that would in 1972 produce the milestone work *The Limits to Growth*. Applying a system dynamics model to map out the growth of population and resources, the study concluded that unless humans altered their trajectory, the planet would face an ecological collapse sometime in the following century. By remarkable coincidence, the study appeared in the same year as a global food shortage broke out, the result of diminished grain harvests in the major breadbaskets of the US, Canada and Australia occurring at the same time as droughts in Africa, South Asia and the Soviet Union. With famine spreading in poor countries and the possibility of global hunger looming, a new alarmism entered popular consciousness.

The choice seemed clear: reduce the population or face doom. In yet another coincidence, the twenty-five-year period of rapid economic growth that followed the Second World War crashed to a juddering halt in 1973 when the oil shock caused by the breakout of war in the Middle East sent energy prices skyrocketing. The rest of the decade would veer between recession and sharply rising prices, accentuating the sudden sense of scarcity that had descended upon the world. It was starting to look like nature might have a kill switch after all.

Reflecting this new pessimism, a bold and wildly innovative theory emerged to argue just that, effectively giving the ancient narrative of a sovereign nature a patina of scientific authority. It began with the understanding that the conditions that made human life possible on planet Earth were extremely finely balanced. Since 1961, scientists had been using the 'Drake equation' to estimate the probability of life on other planets, and concluded that in the entire universe, other civilizations were possible but would be extremely rare. For life to emerge, a star needed to have a planet in the Goldilocks zone – just the right distance from the star to be neither too hot nor too cold – and an atmosphere that would shelter the planet from the most intense rays.

In Earth's case, the atmosphere was sufficiently dense to both retain some of the sun's heat at night while protecting the surface from extreme temperatures at midday, thereby avoiding the sort of boiling days and frigid nights that, say, made life impossible on the moon and other planets. By the late 1950s, climate scientists were growing concerned that human activity might be disrupting this balance. They had long postulated the possibility of a 'greenhouse effect', and now there was growing evidence that the planet's surface temperature was starting to vary outside the normal distribution. They attributed this warming effect to the build-up of gases, particularly carbon, which increased the atmosphere's density enough to allow heat to gradually accumulate in the atmosphere.

Faced with this discovery, the novel Gaia hypothesis thus likened global warming to a fever, suggesting that the earth could be conceived as a living organism that, like our own bodies, had the ability to expel unwanted viruses and parasites (which is what, in the eye of this theory, we'd effectively become). Thus, the environmental shocks that were expected to result from climate change, from extreme weather events like storms and droughts and the forest fires, to an increase in zoonotic epidemics and superbugs, could be seen as the equivalent of the symptoms that accompany human illness when our bodies are trying to exterminate or expel germs: fevers with high temperatures and sweating, vomiting, diarrhoea, and so on.

While easy to grasp, the Gaia hypothesis stirred considerable controversy and was ultimately rejected by most scientists. The consensus opinion was that it was less a hypothesis than a metaphor – useful for understanding, but not testable and falsifiable in the conventional sense. But the science of climate change was now well established and would develop greatly as increasing computer power allowed climate models to become more sophisticated. This in turn enabled scientists to reach more accurate conclusions about the role of human activity in climate change, and to make more accurate predictions about the pace of warming and what its meteorological effects would be.

It was therefore left to the economists to begin estimating what the costs of all this change would amount to. Sadly, for a long time, the profession largely ignored the climate science. Those economists who did take the environment seriously – a relative handful – tended to be those who channelled the spirit of the 1960s. Emphasizing that humans were spiritual as well as material beings, they worried that ecological destruction was inimical to human well-being and mental health, and doubted that more acquisition was the route to happiness. E.F. Schumacher's bestselling 1973 book *Small Is Beautiful*, which embodied such a worldview, carried the subtitle *A Study of Economics as if People Mattered* and advocated an economy based on simplicity and community. Although the ecological economist Herman Daly would eventually make his home at the World Bank, he was the exception for getting a seat in an orthodox institution and remained marginal in the economics establishment of the time.

Given the holistic approach of ecological economics, which involved seeing humans as inseparable from nature – Schumacher integrated Buddhist ethics into his study – their method was not easily digested by a profession that tended towards atomism in its metaphysics. In the 1970s, most of economics was moving in the opposite direction. Following the pioneering work of Milton Friedman on monetary theory and the 'Lucas critique' of the early 1970s, academic economics was shedding what remained of its multidisciplinarity to develop mathematical models of the micro-foundations of human behaviour. As such, it made little time for biology, ethics or the whole-society approach of the macroeconomics that had shaped the discipline until then.

Around this time a new term, 'degrowth', began popping up at the margins of the social scientific literature, often in French publications. The concept was inchoate, floated more as a thought experiment, but when in 1987 the United Nations' Brundtland Commission coined the term 'sustainable development', and the 1992 Rio Earth Summit subsequently called for its operationalization in new ways of measuring gross domestic product, radical economic thinkers began openly challenging the GDP- and growth-focused model of the dominant paradigm. This was particularly the case in France, which was then in the throes of an anti-globalization movement that was busily smashing fast-food outlets. Alongside it, a dissident school of radical economics emerged, taking issue with the celebration of growth. In the same year as the Rio Summit, Wolfgang Sachs published *The Development Dictionary: A Guide to Knowledge as Power*, which was followed two years later by Arturo Escobar's *Encountering Development: The Making and Unmaking of the Third World*. These two books, along with James Ferguson's earlier study of the Lesotho Highlands Dam project,[7] became seminal texts in what came to be called post-development thought. Rather like the postmodern philosophy it borrowed from, this new school of thought questioned the entire development project, arguing it was concerned primarily not with improving human lives but with control – integrating people into the formal, state-managed economy where they could be taxed and monitored.

A simple example illustrates the idea. When I was a child, my mother baked pies. When everyone in my generation grew up, we all went to work, so there was nobody left at home to bake pies; instead, we bought them at the shop on the way home from work. Given that we were all earning money and buying pies, thereby giving work to the baker and shopkeeper, the total output of the economy as recorded in GDP rose by our three incomes. But at the end of the day we still had a pie – and often a pie of inferior quality. Because GDP has risen, that's called progress – progress that can be taxed by the government, while we work in an economy in which we are now dependent on a capitalist employer for employment, and where the quality of some things we consume might even have declined.

Hence the logic of degrowth, which first began to show up in the early 2000s in French scholarly literature[8]: going backwards would weaken both our capitalist employers and the state, but it wouldn't necessarily leave us worse off.

Seek ye first riches, and paradise will follow

In the 1990s, mainstream economists offered a completely different response to the challenges posed by the Brundtland Commission and the Rio Summit. While they no longer ignored the climate, they paid little attention to the radical proposals coming from the left, instead using the standard toolbox of their discipline to propose solutions to the problem. That began with getting the prices right so as to incentivize behavioural change.

I grew up in a small community outside Ottawa, at that time a glorified lumber town that had a side gig as Canada's capital. People from the city used to complain when visitors described it as a backwoods place, but that's what it was – I can still remember being taken to the river as a small boy in the spring to watch the lumberjacks walking across the bed of logs that clogged the floodtide. In those days, whenever we drove into town on the old highway between Ottawa and Montreal, the first four-way intersection we arrived at had a filling station on each corner. Each of them had a garage attached to it where mechanics in coveralls rotated tyres and changed oil and did basic servicing of cars. If we went the other way, towards Montreal, every few miles along the old road we would pass a rustic filling station with a couple of pumps, sometimes with a diner attached or a small family-owned motel next to it.

Today, when I return to visit my Canadian family, I find a city that has grown up into a high-tech hub and engulfed my childhood community. The intersection has become a busy four-lane thoroughfare, the farms have given way to suburban developments and strip malls, the old stone convent in its bucolic riverside setting has been replaced by an industrial-sized nursing home. But despite all that new activity, the intersection now has only one filling station. Its garage has become a convenience store and donut shop. When I drive along the old highways that radiate out of the city, I see abandoned filling stations with pumps overtaken by weeds and dilapidated ghost motels.

It's not that Canadians stopped driving. It's that over time, cars required less petrol. The average fuel economy of cars, measured by the distance one can drive on a litre or a gallon of fuel, roughly doubled between the early 1970s and today.[9] It started in my childhood, around the same time that energy prices soared in the oil shocks of 1973 and 1979. When the price of filling your tank quadrupled, driving a 'boat' with a heavy body and a V8 engine became less a luxury-marker than a signpost of stupidity. Imports and compact models became popular. And as engineers found ways to make engines more efficient, the shift to greater economy in cars became permanent. As a result, there just isn't a need any more for all those petrol stations, and the ecosystem of roadside stops that grew up alongside a technology that demanded frequent stops withered with the disappearance of filling stations that no longer had many customers.

It was just such innovations that gave economists confidence in their models, providing them with the justification to largely ignore talk of an approaching climate crisis. As they anticipated, when a given commodity grew scarce, as oil suddenly had, its price rose; and when its price rose, consumers adjusted their behaviour, using it more efficiently in order to buy less of it. Businesses, themselves on the lookout for new opportunities, were forced to comply lest they lose their customers. And so they searched for new supplies or found ways of extracting existing resources more cheaply until the market got back to balance, or what economists call equilibrium.

It had always been so. Whenever a mineral reserve or area of farmland was depleted, the growing scarcity of its output led buyers to bid up its price. Those rising prices created a money-making opportunity. Anyone who could find new reserves or make existing ones more productive stood to get rich. In response, prospectors would always begin looking for new supplies of minerals, which, lo and behold, is what they would find. Similarly, farmers facing pressures to cut costs would find a way to make their land more productive – say, experimenting with new types of fertilizer or clearing new lands. It thus seemed obvious that more would always come, since more always had. Theoretically, the planet's resources and space were finite, but practically, technology would apparently push these limits to infinity. The same reasoning was applied to pollution. As it increased, citizens would naturally begin to demand a reduction; a premium would thus be attached to clean technologies and then producers, incentivized by the market, would move in that direction.

This belief, that maintaining a free market was the key to solving the environmental crisis, stood in direct opposition to the view that excessive growth was the problem. Instead, it implied that growth was the solution. Although as recently as the late 1980s, as one economist put it, 'relatively few economists have participated in climate change effects research',[10] those who did tended to trust that the sink-or-swim demands of a market economy would generate the adaptations needed to keep the economy growing as the climate changed. Typical of this quiet faith was a late 1980s assessment of American agriculture which predicted that 'with moderate technological change... the productive capacity of U.S. agriculture will likely be greater in seventy-five years than today, even with climate change'.[11]

The climate crisis will make us richer?

Mainstream economists thereby maintained that growth would solve all problems. They called for free markets and globalization to accelerate the transition to a greener future. Pointing to the way Western societies were improving their energy efficiency as they grew richer, they promoted a new idea based on an old rule, the so-called Kuznets curve. Simon Kuznets was a Russian émigré who worked during the Great Depression at the US's National Bureau of Economic Research, where he pioneered the development of national accounting and was instrumental in developing the method used to measure gross national product (GNP). Significantly, though often forgotten, Kuznets warned that 'the welfare of a nation can scarcely be inferred from a measure of national income', and said it was therefore important to work out how that income was distributed before assessing whether growth was progressive or not.[12] By plotting a society's Gini coefficient — an index of income distribution in which 1 represents perfect inequality (one individual receives the entire income of a society) and 0 represents perfect equality (no one individual has any more income than any other individual) — against its GNP at each level of output, Kuznets found a bell-shaped curve. He surmised that in the early stages of the Industrial Revolution, the destruction of the agrarian economy and creation of a landless working class had caused the gains of growth to be captured by an emergent capitalist elite, worsening inequality; but over time, as workers found jobs, labour grew scarce and unions were formed, the rising bargaining power of labour drove up wages, and inequality declined. The same model was then applied to pollution to produce an environmental Kuznets curve — suggesting that in the early stages of the Industrial Revolution pollution rose with output, but beyond a certain threshold the demand for more efficient technology, as happened with automobiles in the 1970s, caused pollution to grow more slowly than output.

Although the environmental Kuznets curve always had a shaky empirical basis, it was eagerly embraced by liberal politicians in the 1990s who paid lip service to social progress and the environment but didn't fancy any talk of sacrifice to improve it, as their predecessors had once done.¹³ 'Environmental preservation will make people richer,' declared US President Bill Clinton, who also said poverty could be eliminated if businesses simply regarded America's most deprived communities as 'untapped markets'.¹⁴ It may have seemed counter-intuitive to say that economic growth both caused and would cure the environmental crisis, but at least economists had now joined the environmental debate. The dominant model was able to accommodate this new way of thinking by treating carbon emissions and their attendant effects on the planet as 'externalities' that the free market would not necessarily rectify on its own, since it amounted to an instance of market failure – something for which neoclassical theory had always allowed. The solution was for the government to set a price on this externality so that producers would then internalize the cost, by means of a carbon tax. By thereby 'getting the price right', the government could create the appropriate incentives, and the free market would do the rest as both consumers and producers looked for the most efficient options.

The search was thus on to find the right price of carbon. In 1992, the American economist William Nordhaus estimated the long-term economic impacts of climate change, which suggested that for every degree of global warming, the world economy would contract by 1–3 per cent, depending on the model.[15] This was a degree of contraction that could pose challenges for policy-makers, but seemed manageable, especially if the global community managed to keep warming to within 1.5 degrees. Nordhaus then worked out that to keep global warming from crossing the 1.5 degree threshold, governments could set a price on carbon of $5 a ton (a price he later raised into the $30–$40 range). Producers would pay this for their pollution, thereby raising the price of more carbon-intensive products and encouraging them and consumers to switch to less polluting products. This, he reckoned, would be sufficient to repair the market failure, and growth could then proceed without further hindrance. Thereafter most economic studies reached conclusions similar to his.

That still left the mitigation costs that would be involved in adjusting to a warming planet. Sea levels would rise, requiring houses to be abandoned and new ones to be built on higher ground. Meanwhile, some parts of the planet would become too dry to support agriculture and would have to be left fallow. Still, most mainstream economists saw growth as the solution, since it would generate the income needed to cover these costs. In a 1994 article that surveyed expert opinion on the impact of climate change, Nordhaus found the economists to be considerably more sanguine than the scientists, thanks to their faith in the 'incredible adaptability of human economies'. One respondent suggested that 'it takes a very sharp pencil to see the difference between the world with and without climate change or with and without mitigation'.[16]

But there would be an inescapable downside. Countries closer to the equator tended to face a bleaker future than those at higher latitudes, since they started with higher average temperatures. And it just so happened that due to the accidents of history – namely, the rise of Europe's empires and their long domination of much of the world – rich countries tended to be clustered in the cooler northern hemisphere whereas those closer to the equator tended to be comparatively poor. What resulted from this legacy was a pernicious rule that those who did the least to cause climate change – the poor countries of the Global South – would suffer the most from its effects, whereas those who did the most to cause it – the rich countries of the West – would suffer least. The University of Notre Dame produces a Global Adaptation Index that ranks the world's countries on their ability to adapt to climate change, assessing both their vulnerability on scores like water and food systems, as well as their social and political 'readiness'.[17] Topping the list as the most able to adapt to climate change are all the world's richest countries, starting with the Scandinavian countries and Switzerland; at the bottom of the list are several African countries, with Chad and the Central African Republic considered the most vulnerable in the world. In some cases, like that of Canada, which on a per capita basis had been one of the planet's very worst climate offenders, most models forecast they'd actually benefit from global warming thanks to longer growing seasons, not to mention lower heating bills.

Thus, mainstream climate economics reclaimed the modern tale, which had appeared threatened by the original ecological studies. Faced with darker narratives that were questioning whether the planet could support human presence indefinitely, their analyses showed that, once again, human ingenuity would triumph over nature. In fact, it was precisely in those nations where science and technology had advanced the furthest – those countries of the Global North that had both caused and would cure the climate crisis – that this triumph would be felt. Those who had been laggards in the entry to the modern age would end up paying the price for their complacency. Nobody said life was fair, but it seemed to reward those who followed the science.

The last shall be last

I first encountered Africa in 1990 when I landed in Abidjan, the capital of Côte d'Ivoire, to start my PhD field research.[18] Côte d'Ivoire had been a success story in the period after it won its independence from France in 1960, its economic growth rate being one of the world's fastest, earning it the moniker of 'Ivoirien miracle'. You could see the markers of that prosperity in Abidjan's impressive skyline – with its high rises, broad boulevards that crossed suspension bridges, the soaring modernist architecture of its cathedral and the luxury of the Hôtel Ivoire, home to West Africa's only indoor skating rink. But, built up over what had once been a fishing village in the prosperous couple of decades after independence, Abidjan had more recently fallen on hard times. During the global recession of the 1970s, prices of its chief exports, cocoa and coffee, had plunged, and the country entered a period of restraint and austerity that had left its mark. The buildings looked mottled with decay, paint faded, plaster peeling, their fountains dry. The hospitals and schools, once beacons of a different future, were crowded, ill-equipped and staffed with overworked doctors and nurses tempted daily by the prospects of greener pastures in rich countries eager for their services. One schoolteacher told me that his classroom, built for thirty students, now packed in sixty.

Such was a typical sight in many capital cities of the developing world in the final decade of the twentieth century. It felt as if, after these countries' heroic efforts to thrust their societies into the modern world, nature had crept back in to reassert its sovereignty – the elements wearing down buildings, the public lawns overgrown, the monuments untended and covered in weeds and vines, heavy rains overwhelming ageing sewer systems. Unlike the derelict petrol pumps on old Canadian highways, abandoned for something better and richer, in the public spaces of many countries in the Global South, the money just seemed to have run out. Economies didn't go backwards in the twentieth century – almost everywhere, they grew after independence. But in much of the developing world they failed to do so fast enough to keep up with the rate of population growth or the breakneck pace of technological change; in some, like Congo and Nigeria, they went through long periods in which incomes actually declined. True, some countries did develop so fast they joined the modern world, particularly in East Asia, with Singapore and South Korea going from being impoverished countries to industrial powerhouses. But in much of Latin America, South Asia, the Caribbean and Africa, the generation that took power after the war often felt as if their work had been left to stagnate or go to seed – as one old Jamaican who'd been involved in independence politics put it simply to me near the end of his life: 'We really missed our chance.'

As it would happen, many of those laggards were, in the course of the 1990s, laying the foundations for what would be dramatic turnarounds in the twenty-first century, with India and China leading the way. But the final decades of the twentieth century left a lingering mark in Western imaginations of a Global South going backwards, producing epic tragedies like the Ethiopian famine of 1984 and the Rwandan genocide of 1994.

The world as a whole, though, was left completely transformed by the half-century after the war. It was richer than ever before, in no small measure due to the unprecedented and immense amount of energy that had been released from the planet's store. And most of that energy was released not by all the humans added to the population of the Global South, but by the relatively small number in the Global North, like the immigrants to Canada and the children they bore, me among them.

Yet those divergent paths would make all the difference as the climate crisis intensified. As the second millennium drew closer to an end, the sort of feedback loops anticipated by the Gaia hypothesis were starting to multiply. Weather was growing more volatile and extreme as a result of what came to be called climate whiplash:[19] global warming would first cause greater evaporation from the soil, resulting in droughts; but that bigger build-up of moisture in the atmosphere would then cause increased rainfall, which in turn produced more abundant vegetation that in the next drought season became vulnerable to wildfires. In consequence, the average number of extreme weather events rose sevenfold.[20] Sea levels were rising, semi-arid areas were turning into deserts, heatwaves were becoming more intense, and surface temperatures kept increasing inexorably.

But while attention was on climate change, the first loop to do major economic damage would take a different form. For decades, the spread of agriculture deep into the forest regions of the developing world had been releasing new zoonotic pathogens into human circulation. Some of the resulting epidemics, like HIV and SARS, were alarming indeed. But these would turn out to be mere trial runs for the most economically devastating one of all in the third decade of the twenty-first century: Covid-19 – the first truly global pandemic, one so grave it would bring the world economy to a standstill. It would reveal how differently the modern world and the one left behind, the bulk of the planet that still lived at the mercy of nature, would fare.

Whereupon the plot would suddenly thicken. The modern tale would begin to look much less like one of unbending advance, and instead begin wending through new twists and turns.

3

THE PANDEMIC PARADOX

In 2020, the world began what amounted to a living experiment. Beset by 'nature's revenge', in the form of a microscopic virus that raced round the world, we would see if the modern tale held true – if, equipped with science and the deep pockets their prosperity made possible, the rich countries of the West could withstand the onslaught and emerge stronger and more dynamic than ever while the poor countries of the developing world underwent carnage, after which their economies and societies would be permanently scarred.

At the start of that year, news bulletins started trickling out of China, reporting an unusual disease outbreak in a Wuhan market. In itself, this wasn't unusual. Zoonotic coronaviruses, like bird flu and SARS, had been coming from that corner of the globe for decades, and this was just the latest.

In February, though, the news darkened. The reports became more frequent and widespread. Flashpoints erupted elsewhere in the world. More infectious than first thought, the virus was moving fast. While it was too soon to say how deadly it would be, that didn't stop the fear-filled chatter online. When images from Italian hospitals of floors crowded with patients conveyed a disease out of control, panic broke out. As Italy locked down, other countries imposed local closures.

At first, those of us in the West were left to fill the information void with our own improvised and chaotic solutions – stockpiling provisions, cancelling appointments, withdrawing cash from ATMs and putting it under mattresses. For me, the relaxed wait for a South African work permit turned urgent. I called the consultant I'd been assigned in Johannesburg, saying I could fly there at once to stay ahead of the lockdown wave that was spreading quickly, and which would soon reach Britain. He told me to sit tight, since South African law didn't permit me to be in the country during the application process. So I waited, and kept watching the news.

The virus continued to spread and by the beginning of March, stock markets were plummeting. Shoppers had now stripped the supermarkets of anything they could find. One after another, public venues closed their doors. On 20 March, with the number of reported cases rocketing in Britain, Prime Minister Boris Johnson declared all remaining public spaces closed. Three days later, he raised that to a full lockdown, ordering everyone to remain indoors. As I was on the phone to my director in Johannesburg, hoping there might be a way for me to work on a temporary contract until the lockdowns lifted, a new bulletin arrived from South Africa: not only was the country closing its borders, but the processing of all work permits would be suspended with immediate effect. My plans went up in smoke. So too did those of millions of others: vacations cancelled, new jobs on hold, house sales suspended, weddings postponed indefinitely.

You could scarcely have asked for a more epic test of the modern tale. Here was exactly the sort of feedback loop the Gaia hypothesis had foretold – a zoonotic virus, locked from time immemorial in a remote forest where it had posed no threat to humans, now released into society as a result of the encroachment of industrial agriculture into the wild, threatening a collapse of the world economy.[1]

It was as if we were witnessing the long-foretold showdown between humans and an angry nature. In the early days we heard lots of stories that echoed a more benign theme of nature 'healing', with images of animals taking over urban streets and talk of bees returning to the city. In my apartment block off a quiet side street in south London, my neighbours and I sat socially distanced on the terraces overlooking the courtyard and did what many Londoners typically avoid doing – we got to know each other, all of us awaiting further instructions on what to do next. The spring of 2020 was an unusually clement one in London so we were able to spend hours sitting on our folding chairs on the terrace, drinking coffee in the day and beer in the evenings, listening to the birdsong we could hear for the first time, hearing a breeze that was usually muffled by the busy traffic or aircraft circling Heathrow in the normally crowded skies. And every evening we'd listen on our mobile phones as the government held its daily news briefing.

Genius to the rescue

What unfolded in the weeks then months that followed would be perhaps the greatest ever version of the modern story. Everything about it, the tragedies and the triumphs, the arc of descent and return, all played out as the tale foretold. Once more, human ingenuity would vanquish nature.

The fifth of humanity living in the world's richest countries would look to their governments to throw up the defences, protect them from the plague, restore their health quickly when they became sick, and then bounce rapidly back to life once the worst had passed. And that's exactly what happened. With their immense stocks of wealth and the access to credit that delivered, governments in the developed world were able to borrow with abandon and open the money spigots: $25 trillion in total, a volume of dollars that if strung end to end would nearly reach the planet Neptune. These governments used this money to build new hospitals, develop vaccines, acquire all the personal protective equipment (PPE) needed to arm their nurses and doctors for battle, and most important of all give us, their citizens, money to pay our bills after they ordered us to stay home from work.

That was what progress had made possible. And we knew, though we seldom spoke about it, that for the mass of humanity in the world least affected by such modern progress, tragedy awaited. For if it was bad in rich countries, the catastrophe that awaited poor ones was sure to be unimaginable. Canada, for instance, entered the pandemic with an estimated five thousand ventilators on hand, an availability similar to other developed countries. South Sudan, in contrast, did so with four. Not four thousand. Four. And if hospitals in rich countries with an average of four to five beds per thousand people were feeling at times overwhelmed – the scenes from Italy so frightened the British government that it mobilized the military to build an entire new hospital just for Covid patients – that could surely only mean catastrophe for the majority of the world's countries where the ratios of beds per thousand patients languished well below one.

Governments in the developing world still proceeded to lock down for fear the pandemic would devastate their population. However, they had no means to give their citizens anything more than a paltry allowance that would perhaps stave off starvation, if that. It stood to reason that their economies would grind to a halt, and it was thus widely expected that people who lived at the margins of existence would get pushed over the edge. Ageing hospitals with shortages of medicines and overworked medical staff would soon be buried under the numbers seen crowding into European wards. Rich countries had locked down the entire global supply of medical equipment, to the point of seizing PPE-laden aeroplanes on foreign runways,[2] and once any of them developed a vaccine, poor countries could be sure that their wealthier neighbours would soak up the supply for their own citizens before offering it for sale at extortionate prices.

Nevertheless, the governments of the Global South had no choice. They told their citizens they would have to face the coming storm largely on their own. Unlike people in rich countries, who were frequently able to retreat into large homes, usually with their own bedrooms, with stocks of food – where they could ride out the storm in relative comfort or even thrive

– those in the Global South withdrew into cramped accommodation in multigenerational households. It was a recipe for healthcare and economic disasters all at once.

Back in the rich countries, what followed was indeed a remarkable testament to the modern tale. Mere weeks into the pandemic, the production of medical equipment shot up fivefold, reducing viral transmission to manageable levels. Just nine months after that, the first vaccines were successfully tested. Within two years, some 12 billion doses had been administered, bringing the modern plague to heel. In due course, despite being faced with the first truly global pandemic in history, humans kept the death toll to an infinitesimal fraction of the great plagues of the past. Whereas between 1346 and 1353 the Black Death had wiped out a third of the population of Europe, Covid-19 killed less than a tenth of a per cent of the world's population. To make it all better, Western countries had set themselves up to bounce back even richer than before. Their citizens, paid to stay at home during lockdowns but with little to spend it on, had put the money aside; the American saving rate rocketed fivefold in 2020 alone. With some $28 trillion, equivalent to a third of global output, injected into the world economy this way, a sea of cash waited to flood the economy once it reopened. The next Roaring Twenties beckoned.

Again, the contrast with the part of the world still at nature's mercy would prove stark. Whereas a Roaring Twenties beckoned for rich countries, economists expected deep scarring for poor ones. At the start of 2022, the International Monetary Fund predicted that whereas the developed countries would return to business as normal, growth in the developing world would end up being 4 per cent lower than it had been before.[3] It couldn't help but be thus: of the $28 trillion added to the world economy, a mere $3 trillion went to the four-fifths of humans who lived in the developing world. Those in the Global South were left to fight for the scraps. For those parts of the world least touched by modernity, therefore, disaster awaited.

By the spring of 2020, with infections soaring in Western countries, investment houses began modelling the course of the pandemic and predicted that by the autumn so many people would have acquired immunity through infection that the pandemic would have peaked, enabling a return to normal life. As one column on Bloomberg put it that summer: 'There's roughly a 60% chance that the countries that have already had a serious outbreak truly have it under control now and that the U.S. will at last subdue it once the Sun Belt surge dies down' and only 'a 20% chance that the worst is yet to come'.[4] Though that prediction didn't age well, since it hadn't taken account of mutations that would produce new strains of the virus and lead to a further lockdown that autumn, the discovery of an effective vaccine late in the year triggered a bout of euphoria. Stock markets rallied, governments would imminently lift the final lockdowns and the party would begin.

But when I reached out to my consultant in Johannesburg, eager to get on a plane to South Africa, I discovered why he'd stopped returning my messages: he had died in the plague. In fact, so many had died or left that the office was reduced to a skeleton crew. The backlog of visas was immense, and it might be years before I would be able to take up my offer. My plans were in tatters and I'd have to start over, making new ones.

Still, I had options. What seemed inescapable, though, was that the world seemed to be heading on two divergent paths: we the lucky ones in the developed world resuming our march forward into a brighter future, the rest of humanity back to a past they had never managed to fully escape. Triumph and tragedy.

A surprise twist in the plot

From the outset, however, something about this narrative of triumph over nature didn't align for me. Having lived so long in the developing world, the picture of an impending catastrophe there seemed too alarmist. I'd seen too many of these predictions for places I'd lived in only to find them unfolding in ways that didn't match the headlines. In particular, having spent many years, on and off in the decades since 1990, living and working in Africa, I'd grown accustomed to Western portrayals of the continent that seemed detached from its reality. Ever since the 1984 Ethiopian famine spurred Western celebrities to organize well-meaning charity events, the continent had come to be portrayed as a backwater in need of Western saviours. Africa is a vastly diverse continent – over fifty countries, some three thousand languages, dizzying ethnic diversity, a mix of both floundering and soaring economies, some of which stood on the cutting edge of digital technology or entertainment – yet the tendency of Western news bureaux to report mainly on conflicts and natural disasters helped to reinforce negative stereotypes.[5] It followed from this premise of a 'lost continent' that the pandemic would devastate a region completely unprepared for it. But at least in some cases, I knew the premise to be wrong.

With time on my hands to think about what the world was going through, I contacted a few colleagues who, like me, had lived in both developing and developed countries over the course of their lives and careers.

Comparing notes, we found ourselves in agreement that the narrative of impending catastrophe in the developing world merited a sceptical eye. We decided to start probing the various changes we believed the world was then undergoing, starting with the question of whether poor countries were in fact turning out to be the biggest victims of the pandemic.

So, in between lockdowns, over several months we went through data sets on income, wealth, Covid-19 diagnoses and excess deaths, and then we began experimenting with some basic regression exercises. Repeatedly we came up with the same result. The modernist thesis, that being rich gave a country a big edge in the pandemic fight, barely found vindication. On balance, rich countries did a little better than poor ones during the pandemic, but not enough to make a substantial difference. Several developing countries were among the worst performing, with Peru, Mexico, Argentina, Libya, South Africa and Bolivia all registering over 500 excess deaths for every 100,000 of the population. But equally, so too did Italy, and several other rich countries weren't far behind, with Britain, the US and Portugal at well over 400. And while several developed countries were among the star performers, with Denmark and Australia producing death rates well below 200, more than a dozen African countries also fell below that threshold.

Moreover, even the modest advantage that rich countries on average enjoyed in keeping down death rates was quickly wiped out by the inordinately higher cost they had to bear for that tiny edge: the $25 trillion combined spend in the West and China worked out to a per capita cost of roughly $7,000, whereas for citizens in the rest of the world the per capita cost of fighting the pandemic came to a less than princely sum of roughly $575. Relatively speaking, therefore, the cost of staying alive was some twelve times higher in rich countries than poor ones.

Breaking the data into sub-groups didn't make the results any less murky. Comparatively poor Latin America did badly; but so too did comparatively rich Europe. Within Europe, the poorer countries, particularly former communist states – Bosnia and Herzegovina at 796, North Macedonia at 826, Serbia at 857 and Bulgaria at 965 per 100,000 – did badly while many richer ones did well. Scrambling everything, therefore, was the fact that some of the planet's worst performers were among its richest countries, while the league table of star performers, which is to say those countries that kept their death rates very low, was filled with African countries that numbered among the poorest countries in the world. For its part, South Sudan, with its paltry four ventilators, came in at 186 deaths per 100,000, far below the dire prognostications at the outset of the pandemic.[6]

Data quality didn't explain away what was a surprising finding. While it's plausible that many deaths from Covid-19 might not have been recorded in poor countries because their health systems lacked the diagnostic capacity to identify them, excess deaths do eventually show up in the data, giving a more reliable indicator. On balance, therefore, it was hard not to reach the conclusion that there was apparently no advantage to being in a rich country during the pandemic – and when it came to the price tag, the richer a country was, the more it had to spend to keep its citizens safe.

We pondered various possible explanations for this seeming paradox. Part of it may have come down to the relative youth of the developing world. The median age in Europe is about forty-five, a bit higher than North America, while in Japan it's fifty. In South Asia and South America, in contrast, it's closer to thirty, while in Africa it's barely twenty. It's not a given that young people are always going to be more resistant to disease than elderly populations, but on average they bounce back from sickness more quickly than the elderly, just as they bounce back more quickly from injury. (Trust me on this: I used to box with my sons when they were teenagers, and I'm still recovering.)

Some of it may have come down to the fact that, particularly in Africa, being less developed economically and industrially meant countries were also less urbanized. In the developed countries, between 75 per cent and 80 per cent of the population live in cities.[7] In developing countries, it's often less than a half, and in the poorest countries it's still around only a quarter. The wide dispersion of the population thus made transmission less of a problem than in the crowded communities of the world's richest cities. But this explanation could take us only so far, since in the cities of poor countries, the population tends to be extremely densely packed, making risks to urban populations far higher.

Another factor probably came down to the long experience many developing countries, particularly in Africa, already had in dealing with zoonotic pandemics.[8] HIV and Ebola had already primed Africans for the threat nature could pose, so the citizenry was already versed in the mitigation measures used to limit contagion, such as social distancing, temperature checking and handwashing, and were quick to cooperate when officials called for them to do so. In fact, even before lockdowns were announced, citizens in many developing countries had already taken to wearing masks. Equally, in many African airports, arriving travellers already passed through a quick fever scan in immigration lines (often without realizing it), so retooling to test for Covid was comparatively easily done. It also didn't hurt that the virus had spread first from China to developed countries, giving authorities in the developing world a precious few more days to anticipate and prepare for what was coming.

But all this explained only how some poor countries did well. It didn't account for the many failures among rich countries. There appeared to be something else going on too, and I'd actually had my first inkling of it many years earlier. The incident came back to me as I looked at how our world was being turned upside down.

'Know the enemy and know yourself'

Back in 2002, at a time when I was living and working in Jamaica, I was preparing for the birth of my daughter. She was to be delivered at a hospital where her godmother-to-be was then doing her medical residency, and while the staff there were well-trained and devoted practitioners, I still would not have wanted us to encounter any significant complications at her birth. Though rich in talent and human resources, Jamaica remained a poor country and its hospitals betrayed that: bare concrete walls, rusted dangling ceiling fans for airflow, a relatively limited range of medicines, modern equipment that was nonetheless well shy of the technological frontier. For most births, what was available would be more than sufficient; but in those rare cases that required advanced interventions, we might have desperately missed the hospitals of the developed world.

Fortunately, our daughter arrived in perfect health and the hospital was more than sufficient for our needs. We were thus able to take her home on a sunny Jamaican autumn morning, the pink hibiscus radiant in the morning light.

But just a few days later, I was surprised by a rapping at my front gate. When I went out onto the verandah to see who it was, yelling out my reply to the callers that we didn't have dogs, two young women in nurses' uniforms entered the yard. Making their way into the house, they announced they were there to see the baby. I hadn't been told to expect anyone and as they proceeded to open their bags and pull out a portable scale and other medical instruments I asked if there was a problem. They told me there wasn't, that everything was fine and they were from the ministry, where they had been forwarded the details of my daughter's arrival. It turned out every baby born in the country's hospitals received the same treatment.

Throughout the island, villages are equipped with health centres from which such nurses operate, delivering primary healthcare – checking vital signs, monitoring physical conditions and signs of poor nutrition, charting children's progress against normal rates, all to ensure a citizenry that is as healthy as possible. It's a big part of the reason why Jamaica, whose per capita income is less than 15 per cent of the US's, has an average life expectancy not far different from its much richer neighbour – 71 years as opposed to 78. This allocation of medical resources towards primary care is typical of many developing countries, reflecting a philosophy that if you can't provide your citizens with luxury healthcare, you can at least ensure they get the basics right.

As a rule, the share of a country's health spending allocated to primary care rises as its per capita income declines. Thus, some poor countries allocate as much as 90 per cent of their expenditure to primary care;[9] some of the world's richest countries spend less than a quarter of that, in percentage terms.[10] If poor countries can't do much for you if you develop a serious malady, like various forms of cancer or rare complications, at least they'll do what they can to ensure you don't end up in hospital. An ounce of prevention is worth a pound of cure.

This reflects a basic reality of life in a poor country. Whereas in rich countries the main causes of death are illnesses of longevity like cardiovascular diseases and cancer, in poor countries the big killers most often target infants and small children, with diarrhoeal diseases being especially prevalent. Thus, simple and relatively inexpensive interventions become vital: seeing that the babies are born healthy and don't show early signs of trouble, as my two nurses did with my daughter, and teaching the basics of good practice and hygiene to the population from a young age. When it comes to diarrhoeal diseases, for instance, much of the best prevention comes down to good primary health and hygiene practices.[11]

Accordingly, when you live in a developing country, you quickly learn and internalize a suite of practices that reduce the incidence of what are usually minor but can become fatal infections: regular handwashing or sanitizing, boiling and filtering water, using straws and inspecting dishes and cutlery carefully in restaurants, never allowing grocery bags to touch the ground, scrutinizing produce and meat in markets and washing them before preparation once back home (even peeled fruit gets washed, since the knife piercing a skin could pick up microbes on its way through the flesh), frequent use of disinfectants when cleaning kitchen surfaces or whatever objects are handled by a sick family member. All of this not only serves the needs of primary health, but helps compensate for the relative thinness of state controls on safety and hygiene: even though there are health and safety regulations, you don't trust resource-strapped enforcers to guarantee them and so you develop your own compensating mechanisms, just in case.

In spite of all these practices, especially when you live in the tropics, you still can't eliminate infection altogether – though, curiously, this may actually offer further advantages. Growing up in the tropics, my children had the occasional battles with dengue fever, 'running belly' or minor stomach worms, all of which would be treated quickly with rest and tea – there's nothing a West Indian won't try to cure with tea – and simple medicines. But the incidence and severity of such infections were thereby reduced to the point that they seldom rose beyond the level of minor inconveniences – at most, a day off school (making these ailments a positive attraction to the children). The balance that resulted seems to land in a sort of sweet spot: hygiene practices that reduced severe infection to a minimum, coupled with sufficient minor illness to keep the body's immune system primed more than might be the case in comparatively sanitized rich countries.

What can't be overstated enough is how these small gestures, done many times a day, every day of one's life, shape one's thinking. In particular, they instil a high regard for the threats that abound in nature. Even in benign environments like the Caribbean, where exposure to nature consists largely of abundant sun or bounteous fruit, the knowledge that something beautiful could nonetheless harbour a menacing edge is ingrained in popular consciousness. After all, the same beautiful island everyone inhabits can suddenly be ravaged pitilessly by a hurricane, as was the case with Hurricane Melissa in October 2025.

So when the pandemic reached the developing world, whether or not their governments were prepared, societies most often were. Between good primary healthcare and rapidly activated community support groups, they stood ready to meet the challenge headed their way. Sitting in London at the outbreak of the pandemic, therefore, I felt rather serene about the prospects of my many friends and associates in the developing world, notwithstanding the predictions of a carnage that was supposedly about to befall them. While they were obviously concerned, they also knew this script already.

It was what was happening around me that troubled me.

The pride before a fall

The first hints something would go wrong came in the very earliest days of the pandemic. On 27 February 2020, a day after saying the US had fifteen cases of coronavirus that would soon drop to zero, President Donald Trump opined, 'It's going to disappear. One day – it's like a miracle – it will disappear.'

Four days later in London, standing next to his chief medical officer as they addressed the nation, Prime Minister Boris Johnson said he'd just visited a hospital with coronavirus patients and that while there 'I shook hands with everybody, you will be pleased to know, and I continue to shake hands.' The message coming out of such capitals, in short, was that there was nothing to worry about. As Johnson would say a few months later, prematurely declaring the pandemic largely vanquished and reopening pubs and restaurants – a measure that would lead to a new round of infections and force a second lockdown – 'We have the world's most brilliant medical minds, the world's best pharmaceutical companies, our doctors and treatments are the best in the world.'[12]

In fact, the US and the UK would go on to be among the countries with the worst outcomes during the pandemic. A new concept then entered the public domain – that for all their wealth, resources and scientific advancement, when faced with a major ecological shock, their societies lacked *resilience*. Was that somehow connected to the hubris they had shown in believing that their societies' science and wealth would enable them to brush off the virus as a temporary inconvenience?

Before the pandemic, resilience had been a topic of interest mainly to academics and policy wonks. For decades until then, reflecting the dominant neoliberal model of economic organization, the lodestar of both politics and policy in Western countries had been efficiency: maximum revenue at minimum cost. For example, just-in-time inventory management kept orders for goods sold by retailers or inputs in a factory to just a few days' supply, thereby reducing warehousing costs: you placed your next order 'just in time' for the current stock's depletion. Similarly, instead of doing everything in-house, manufacturers moved towards globally distributed supply chains: spreading the production process across many suppliers in other countries enabled a plant manager not only to buy the best and best-priced products, but to shift production quickly to another supplier if one went offline (for instance, due to a strike or power failure). All of this became possible in a world in which trade, people and information flowed freely, something that the collapse of the Soviet bloc, China's opening to the world and the end of global bipolarity made possible. 'We've become global citizens,' wrote the Japanese management consultant Kenichi Ohmae in 1989, on the eve of the fall of the Berlin Wall, 'and so must the companies that want to sell us things.'[13] By such means did companies eliminate perceived waste to make themselves lean, mean and efficient.

But reducing waste had an unanticipated side effect. It came to light in 2020 when the global shipping industry suddenly froze. Shortages erupted and there was talk that some import-dependent countries might now even starve. A new holy grail then came along to replace that of efficiency: resilience. An August 2021 survey of corporate executives by KPMG found an overwhelming desire to 're-think their approach to supply chains in order to become more agile, as well as bringing production closer to home and making their supply chain more robust'.[14] And when it came to societies, Covid-19 was going to test societal resilience as few shocks had ever done, with many rich societies found to be wanting.

Defined as 'the magnitude of disturbance that a system could tolerate and still persist', resilience first entered the social scientific literature from ecology.[15] Unlike ecological resilience, which was seen as the ability of an ecosystem to restore stability amid change, social resilience was generally understood to be the ability to return to a previous equilibrium after a shock, with possible adaptations along the way that would then improve future resilience.[16] When first applied to the study of societies, scholars tended to assume that to be rich was to be resilient, since much of the original literature assumed a key aspect of resilience to be the ability to access resources via either the state or civil society.[17]

For example, in his book *Searching for Safety*, Aaron Wildavsky contrasted two strategies for managing risk: anticipation and resilience.[18] Anticipation required looking ahead to the possible risks that might arise and then putting in place the defences that would make it possible to deal with any threats once they arose – so, for instance, in preparing for a possible pandemic, that entailed building stockpiles of medicine, equipping hospitals, training doctors and nurses, and so forth. Resilience, in contrast, involved a certain degree of resignation to the fact that a society couldn't prepare for all risks, and so the best it could hope to do was be strong and flexible and respond to any challenge that arose as best it could. It went without saying that anticipation, which required bureaucratic foresight and the commitment of resources to meet demands that might not even materialize, was costly, making it a coping strategy that only developed countries could use. But having those resources meant that, when threats arose, rich countries were prepared, ultimately making them more resilient – even though resilience was not the strategy they employed. Poor countries were left to get by as best they could, as happened during the pandemic.

But as we've seen, on balance, rich societies emerged from the pandemic no better than poor societies did, though the anticipation strategies on which they relied consumed immense amounts of resources, ultimately saddling them with considerable debts. Curiously, poor countries may have enjoyed an advantage in a resource that was cheap and inexhaustible: the high regard for the pandemic's threat, which led people to eschew the sort of hubris expressed by some Western leaders and parts of their citizenries. In developed countries, an unintended by-product of long histories of government action that succeeded in minimizing threats may have been a complacency among some residents that led them not to take a new threat sufficiently seriously. That might explain why a significant minority in rich countries resisted protocols such as distancing and mask wearing as infringements on their liberty.[19]

It would also align with recent studies that have found that overestimating one's ability to cope with the effects of climate change makes people more vulnerable to its effects, a topic we'll return to later.[20] The economist Hyman Minsky actually had a theory to explain a similar phenomenon in economics, namely that long periods of financial stability induced a complacency about the risks of a financial crisis recurring, the result being that politicians and regulators began to lighten their touch or investors took greater risks on new products until ultimately they provoked a new financial crisis. What Minsky said of the economy, that 'success breeds a disregard of the possibility of failure',[21] could just as well be said of societies. Put differently, a truth of human existence may be that pride frequently precedes a fall.

Much resilience appears to be born of necessity, particularly the necessity to compensate for the very absence of modernity's benefits – the natural inclination towards caution regarding germ transmission in environments where disease is common, precautionary approaches to hygiene in places where sanitary enforcement is lax, the readiness to rapidly alter behaviours when faced with an external threat, and so forth. When all is said and done, it may be that there's still something to be said for living if not at the mercy of nature, at least conscious of its threat; that societies which have managed to persuade themselves that they have risen beyond nature can leave themselves unprepared for its revenge, whatever form that takes. In short, it appears that as a society grows rich and increasingly insulates itself from the vagaries of nature, the behaviour of its citizens changes in such a way as to raise the cost of the society's resilience when faced with natural shocks.

Even so, despite the enormous cost exacted on them by the pandemic, rich countries came through it and were set up to bounce back relatively quickly. The immense pool of savings accumulated throughout multiple lockdowns was ready to revive the economy. The new Roaring Twenties lay ahead.

4

THE WEALTH PARADOX

The second part of the living experiment was now to begin. We would see if the recovery from the pandemic advanced more quickly in rich countries than poor ones, leaving the latter to trail behind desperately, like slow runners in a race.

Very early in the outbreak, a view took hold among economists that once Western governments wrestled the pandemic under control, the economy would rocket back to life. It seemed inevitable. Throughout multiple lockdowns, everyone had been counting the days until they could return to their favourite pubs, bars and restaurants, join others in theatres and cinemas, visit barbers or stylists to freshen up their appearance, go shopping and take holidays again. Having placed as much as a third of their income in savings accounts when almost everywhere was closed and there was little to spend it on, they had plenty of disposable cash. It followed that all this spending would create so much demand in the economy that employers would hire new workers to fill the orders, and those new employees would then have new incomes with which to create yet more demand. Companies would make so much money off this boom that their share prices would soar, enriching ordinary people further and prompting them to spend yet more, in a virtuous upward spiral that could conceivably go on for years.

When economies reopened for business in 2021, they fulfilled the economists' predictions and returned, Lazarus-like, to life. The American economy grew 6.1 per cent that year, France's by 6.9 per cent and Britain's a whopping 8.6 per cent – rates of expansion not seen in a century. Not seen, that is, since the original Roaring Twenties.

But then, just as quickly as they'd bounced back, the developed economies settled back down to their previous languor.[1] By 2023, most of them were close to stagnant, their combined average growth in per capita GDP barely reaching a paltry 1 per cent that year – far below their historical average of over 2 per cent, which itself was a retreat from the torrid 5–6 per cent pace that had followed the Second World War. In fact, once one subtracted new debt from new economic output, they were pretty much standing still.[2] To cap it all off, after factoring in population growth and adjusting for inflation, what transpired was that real GDP per capita had peaked in most developed countries just before the pandemic and that afterwards, a funk settled in. In Japan,[3] income growth barely inched upwards; it remained flat in France,[4] Germany[5] and the United Kingdom;[6] and in Canada,[7] it began going backwards.

There was, however, one Western country that kept alive the dream of this renaissance for a while, and that was the United States. Through 2023, while all its G7 peers struggled with stagnation, the US economy continued expanding at a rate of nearly 3 per cent a year, maintaining the trend of the decade before the pandemic. Amid suggestions of a new American golden age, this one was built on artificial intelligence (AI) rather as the original gilded age had been built on railways, euphoria gripped the stock market, with investors from all over the world rushing in to ride the boom. The resulting surge went so far that at its peak in 2024 the US stock market accounted for half the value of all the world's publicly traded companies. The so-called Magnificent Seven, those big companies in the vanguard of the revolution in AI – Alphabet, Amazon, Apple, Meta, Microsoft, Nvidia and Tesla – were at that point together worth more than the stock markets of every other country on the planet. Nvidia alone became so valuable that its market capitalization eventually surpassed what Canada's entire economy produced that year.

But this 'American exceptionalism' was always something of an illusion. Fundamentally, the country was suffering from the same ailment of stagnating growth besetting other Western economies. Unlike everyone else, though, it was able to medicate its way through the gloom with the one thing allowed to it by what a French finance minister had once called its 'exorbitant privilege' – the fact that the dollar was the world's principal reserve currency. That meant the American government could always find buyers for the Treasury bonds it sold to finance its spending, essentially allowing it to borrow endlessly. It did so enthusiastically. The US's national debt had risen sevenfold[8] since the turn of the millennium and during the pandemic and the post-pandemic rebound, from 2020 to 2024, a time when the American economy added $6.6 trillion to its annual output,[9] the country added another $11.6 trillion to its national debt.[10] In other words, all its growth was borrowed – and then some. Unlike during the postwar golden age, when each dollar of national debt had, through multipliers, added $10 to national output, now the return was 50 cents.[11] Had the country lived within its means and not used any further credit, it would thus have been going backwards. Which meant that if and when the debt binge stopped, so would the economy.

It was just a matter of time before this scheme began to test creditor patience. By 2024, amid forecasts from the Congressional Budget Office that the national debt would rise endlessly,[12] strains began to show in American markets: bond yields were rising and gold prices were setting new records as investors began retreating from US Treasury paper and into the safe haven of the shiny ancient metal. The rest of the world was still willing to lend to the US, but was now starting to demand higher interest rates to do so.

Further headwinds to the American boom came with the start of 2025 and the return of Donald Trump to the White House. Within weeks of his inauguration, his administration rolled out a chaotic and unpredictable set of policies that unsettled markets. It started with a head-scratching list of tariffs on all the world's countries that, it soon emerged, had been compiled by an AI chatbot. (This might help to explain why the list included countries that didn't exist, like the island occupied entirely by penguins – which the administration subsequently insisted was included 'just in case'.) This so-called Liberation Day was soon followed by a series of rapid rollbacks and carve-outs to the tariffs, followed by their reimposition on some countries whose governments had irritated Trump in one way or another. Some companies were then made to pay special contributions or make policy changes lest Washington target them for punishment, though CEOs could sometimes mollify the president's demands with obsequious presentations of gifts and tributes.

None of this did anything to improve the business environment. Although the stock market continued rising on the AI boom, the rest of the economy began to stumble. But while Trump would then be blamed for knocking back an otherwise healthy economy, the deceleration would likely have happened anyway. From the moment the *Financial Times* opened the new year with a headline trumpeting 'Davos hits "peak pessimism" on Europe as US exuberance rises',[13] the signs were there that the best was past: market traders know such peaks of pride always presage a fall. Within days the dollar index – a proxy for the net flow of global funds into the US – reached its multi-year peak, and then began a steady decline that would continue through the year. Investors, who had crowded in from all around the world to ride the US boom, were now pulling in their horns and shifting their focus elsewhere. Thus, even before Trump took office, quietly but unmistakably, European, Asian and many emerging-market stock markets had begun to outperform the US one.[14] As its economic downturn finally brought the US back closer to the club of sluggish economies, it ceased to be all that exceptional.

Even more surprising than the fizzling out of the rapid but brief economic rebound from the pandemic was the geographic composition of the global growth that remained. In stark contrast to expectations of a sharp rebound in Western countries coupled with deep scarring in the developing world, the reverse happened: it was the economies of the erstwhile global periphery that leapt from the blocks. In India in 2024, there was nearly 7 per cent growth. This was higher in Vietnam, and higher still in Benin and Niger, both of which grew that year by more than 8 per cent.[15]

It was easy enough for anyone to overlook this, given the strong variation in performance among developing countries. The very poorest were, in many cases, hit hard, ending much of the world's progress in human development (the measure that factors in how growth translates into improvements in well-being, measured by such things as income and education).[16] Meanwhile, Africa's overall performance was skewed downwards by the fact that a disproportionate share of the world's fragile and conflict-affected states are currently located in a belt across the middle of the continent,[17] with countries like Chad, Sudan and the Central African Republic sinking so far that their per capita incomes dropped below their already desperately low levels in 2024.[18]

However, many other countries across the developing world, which had already begun steady rises up the income ladder, rebounded mightily. India, Cambodia, Ethiopia and Rwanda, to name just a few that had crossed the threshold into steady growth, were rising at rates that, if sustained, would double their people's incomes every dozen or so years. Those many strong performances thus lifted the average rate of growth in the developing world. On the whole, consequently, developing countries recovered quickly from the 2020 pandemic recession and then kept growing strongly. By 2025, whereas few developed economies were growing faster than 1 per cent a year, the average rate in the developing world surpassed 4 per cent.[19]

Although the epicentre of global dynamism shifted somewhat, away from China and towards India and South East Asia, China still managed to grow at nearly 5 per cent per year – a rate that, if slower than before, was nonetheless the envy of Western countries. Moreover, the rise of the Global South had gone beyond being a purely Asian story. By the time the recovery was in full swing in 2022, several countries in Africa and Latin America were expanding at annual rates approaching 10 per cent. Niger, Guyana and the Philippines led the pack with double-digit growth, while of the twenty fastest-growing economies in 2024, eleven were in Africa,[20] the continent meant to have been devastated by the pandemic. This was not new, as many of these economies had begun growing strongly before the pandemic; what was surprising, though, was that whereas Western countries struggled to recover, many developing ones resumed their prior growth rates seemingly unscathed.

The reversal of fortunes was thus even more dramatic than it had been during the pandemic. Then, being rich brought a country no advantage in fighting the plague. But afterwards, it appeared that being rich was more than irrelevant; it seemed a positive handicap. As the richer countries struggled to emerge from their economic gloom, many of the poorer ones took off, with some of the poorest among them turning into the star performers of the world economy. It was as if a Mercator map had been turned upside down, giving an entirely new shape to the world.

It was all rather puzzling, even bewildering, to a good many economists.

What killed the Roaring Twenties?

So what happened? What came along to pre-empt the new Roaring Twenties we'd been led to expect?

There was always something a little too neat about the parallels between the 1920s and the 2020s. Yes, in both periods an international epidemic presaged a stock market boom, but beyond those similarities the decades bore little resemblance to one another. For starters, the West in 1920 was the unrivalled centre of the global economy, still ascendant and near the peak of its power. Though they were encountering greater opposition in their colonies, Europe's empires were still expanding their reach. Nobody rivalled them militarily, and the US was still in the early stages of what would be a long rise to eventual global domination. In short, the best years of the West still lay ahead.

And they did so because a century ago the Western world was much younger than it is today – both literally and figuratively. In the US, for instance, the median age in 1920 was twenty-five, whereas today it's approaching forty.[21] The US isn't even particularly representative of most developed countries since it has always been able to keep its population younger than most by importing workers. Most advanced economies have historically been more uncomfortable with mass immigration than the US (and the US, it bears noting, is itself now becoming more unfriendly to immigrants). But take Japan, for instance, a country that has always had a fairly restrictive approach to immigration.[22] In 1920, nearly two-fifths of its population was under fifteen, whereas today that figure is only one in eight. All told, a century ago the dependency ratios in Western countries – which is to say, the share of the population not working – was about similar to today's, but with a crucial difference. Back then, most of the economically inactive population were children who consumed resources they would later repay once they entered the workforce, leaving roughly 5 per cent of the population retired. Today, the latter figure is closer to 20 per cent, with Japan being at the extreme, with nearly one in every three of its citizens today being pensioners.[23]

While the elderly have done their part for society, very few will ever re-enter the productive economy. Thus, in the 1920s, there was far more latent energy ready to get moving as the money poured in and the children grew up to become workers. Figuratively, too, the West was younger than it is today in that most people still had little more than primary education. The significance of this can be found in the economics of education: there's evidence of diminishing returns in education spending, meaning you get the most bang for your buck in the early stages of a person's formation.[24] If you take someone who is illiterate and give them basic literacy and numeracy, it can lead to major improvements in their productivity – apart from anything else, they can read an instruction manual and do simple calculations – and such large returns on education spending continue through secondary school. Thus, in the decades after 1920, because secondary education went from being a minority to a majority status across Western societies, it greatly raised the productivity of the population. In addition, with university education still confined to a fairly small share of the population, most people entered the workforce in their teen years and so would end up contributing to the nation's economic output for nearly five decades, if not more. To add further fuel to the economic fire, all these young people were starting gainful employment as one of the great productivity-enhancing revolutions, electrification, was in full swing. This combination of factors meant that over the next few decades, labour productivity would rise at unprecedented rates, leading to sustained and rapid economic growth, which reached its height in the three decades after the Second World War. At that time, when the soldiers returned home and all the children of the 1920s and 1930s entered the workforce, Western countries grew at average annual rates of 5–6 per cent per year, living standards doubling every dozen or so years as a result.

None of these conditions applied at the end of the Covid-19 pandemic. The roughly 20 per cent retirement rate constrained the ability to ramp up output similar to the era when most people were working or soon to work. Moreover, with nearly half of the population,[25] on average, attaining university degrees,[26] people today enter the workforce later and, in many countries, retire earlier. Add to this life expectancies that have greatly improved – on the cusp of the 1920s, the average life expectancy across Western countries stood below fifty,[27] whereas now it's approaching eighty – and today a growing share of the population in some countries actually spends as little as a third of their life in gainful employment. That means a higher share of the economy's output must be oriented towards consumption, leaving less for business investment. Finally, despite constant hope that new technologies like the computer, the Internet or AI will cause the sort of productivity revolution that electricity and the steam engine did in their day, the long-term trend in the West's labour productivity growth has been moving relentlessly downwards for decades, and still shows no signs of ever turning back up.[28]

That may be in part due to the more concentrated productivity impacts of today's technological innovations. There's no question that social media, for instance, has revolutionized society – possibly for the worse, to judge from recent research on its mental health impacts[29] or its fostering of political polarization. However, there's little evidence of it raising labour productivity across the economy. Whereas electricity raised everyone's productivity, from butchers to barbers to doctors, technological innovations today tend to raise the productivity only within some industries, and not across the economy. While the Internet may have made delivery services more efficient, barbers can't cut hair any quicker as a result. Instead, what tends to happen today is that technological changes take hold in a small number of companies, which then drive competitors out of business, raising the average productivity in that sector but doing less to alter economy-wide output.[30]

This was the changed context into which the pandemic-era stimulus was injected. Rather than fuel an investment boom, most of the money was required just to keep economies afloat. Despite that, Western economies still contracted. Developed countries borrowed as much as a quarter of their GDP to support their economies through the lockdowns yet still suffered contractions of 5–10 per cent of GDP. In other words, had they not borrowed so heavily, their economies would have lost as much as a *third* of their output, which would have been a scale of contraction never before seen in the industrial age outside of war. Developing countries, by contrast, deprived of deep pools of capital, borrowed very little – a mere $3 trillion of the $28 trillion pandemic debt, far below their share of more than half the planet's population – yet experienced contractions that were muted by comparison, being on average shallower than those in Western countries.

This has been a little-discussed feature of the wealth of Western economies: that as they grow richer, the amount of money governments must inject during economic downturns goes up. Since the 1980s, the amount Western governments have spent in fiscal and monetary stimulus during recessions has risen from an average 1 per cent of GDP to 12 per cent at the time of the 2008 global financial crisis and a whopping 35 per cent at the time of the pandemic.[31] But while these rapid responses have made recessions less frequent and less deep, they've done nothing to restore the health of the economies. On the contrary, the average annual growth rate of Western economies has continued remorselessly downwards all the while, and is now approaching zero.

Which makes one wonder, is there something about growing rich that slows an economy?

The wealth paradox

Although the economic slowdown in the West became stark in the wake of the pandemic, it pre-dated the lockdowns. Indeed, its origins can be traced back to half a century ago. For roughly a quarter-century after the Second World War, the global economy went through the fastest growth in the history of humanity, tripling in size. To put that in context, since the dawn of the Industrial Revolution in the eighteenth century, when after millennia of near-stagnation the world economy took off, it had grown roughly twenty-five times over. Most of this spectacular expansion occurred in the brief golden age following the war.

By the late 1960s, though, the boom was beginning to fade. In that decade, the annual growth rate of global per capita GDP had averaged over 3 per cent.[32] In subsequent decades, it would never approach this figure. Initially, though, this was due to a slowdown not of the rich economies but of the poor ones. When most of Europe's remaining colonies gained their independence after the war, they adopted import substituting (IS) policies to accelerate their industrialization, insulating local manufacturers from foreign competition with protective barriers like tariffs, import quotas and licences while borrowing to build infrastructure. But by the 1970s, the IS model had run its course. Once their domestic markets were supplied with local products, economies were left saddled with inefficient firms, rising debts and slowing growth. The loss of dynamism became so stark that the 1980s in Africa came to be known as the 'lost decade' for development. Although the world economy as a whole grew more slowly, this quicker deceleration of the developing countries meant that the share of global output consumed by a relative handful of Western countries grew even larger, peaking at about four-fifths at the turn of the millennium.

However, by the 1990s, developing countries had largely scrapped their IS strategies for export-oriented reform, led by two hitherto-poor countries that would subsequently become industrial powerhouses, China and

India. China's reform had begun in the late 1970s when Deng Xiaoping, declaring that 'socialism cannot endure if it remains poor', began a gradual but ultimately radical transformation of the economy from state control to a market economy under Communist Party guidance. India followed suit when in 1991 its finance minister, Manmohan Singh, introduced a radical programme to dismantle state direction of the economy, quoting Victor Hugo when he announced his plans to parliament: 'No power on earth can stop an idea whose time has come.' After the turn of the millennium, the distribution of global growth then changed: the developed countries began to decelerate, sharply so after the 2008 financial crisis, while developing countries raced ahead. Within twenty years, that four-fifths of global output consumed by Western countries had already fallen to three-fifths. So, whereas in 1980, India's per capita income had been roughly a thirtieth of the United Kingdom's, four decades later it was less than a twentieth; China's rise was even more spectacular, going from a fortieth of British incomes to a quarter in the same time period.[33]

This did not come as a surprise to me. I was living and working in the developing world throughout this time and could see what was happening. My work on the global economy and the rise of its erstwhile periphery ultimately led me into a collaboration with the historian Peter Heather, out of which came our theory of imperial life cycles: that empires grew rich and powerful off the exploitation of their colonial peripheries, but in the process inadvertently developed those peripheries until they acquired the capacity to resist and then eventually reverse imperial domination. The main difference we identified between antiquity and the modern period was that the imperial competition that brought about the fall of the Roman Empire unfolded on the battlefield, whereas in the modern period it took place mainly in trade and diplomacy.

Yet our model specified that, unlike what happened to the Roman Empire, the decline of the modern West remained relative. Its share of the world economy would continue declining but its economic output could continue rising, just more slowly than that of the erstwhile periphery, which would eventually catch up to it. The model said nothing about the continued slowing of the world economy, nor about the actual reversal of Western economies. Once the pandemic ended, some Western countries unexpectedly started going backwards – which is to say, per capita income began falling. From an admittedly high plateau, the citizens of some Western countries were literally getting poorer. That was something Peter and I hadn't anticipated, and it required a new theory.

The idea that poor countries would grow faster than rich ones isn't novel to economists. While there is some debate about this, the neoclassical growth model that still dominates economics presumes that poorer countries will grow faster than rich ones, and so will eventually converge with them. The so-called Solow-Swan model, which Robert Solow and Trevor Swan developed independently of one another in 1956, started from the premise that application of a new technology would raise labour productivity, but that eventually the returns on continually adding the technology would diminish. This gave an incentive to investors, governments and business managers to then move the technology to areas where it didn't yet exist, namely poorer regions and countries, where the returns on the investment would be higher. It followed from this that poor countries would eventually converge with rich ones in their per capita income.

By the late twentieth century, though, only a handful of developing countries had actually reached rich-country status. This led some economists to qualify the model by saying countries needed to put the right conditions in place to converge – 'It's the politics, stupid!' wrote the economist Dani Rodrik in his comments on the seminal book *Why Nations Fail* by his colleagues Daron Acemoglu and James Robinson, which argued that the right institutions were necessary before a country could ride the wave of global development.

Other economic models, like the so-called endogenous growth school, went further yet and argued that technology could enable rich countries to maintain their lead indefinitely, because new technology sprang from knowledge and innovation, at which rich countries excelled. Paul Romer pointed out that ideas were 'non-rival', meaning that, unlike people or resources, an idea could be used infinitely without added strain on the natural environment. In his 2018 address upon winning the Nobel Prize in Economics for his work on endogenous theory, Romer cited the example of the humble gas mantle, which magnified the light of a flame ten times over, using it to illustrate the point that the application of new ideas could itself raise output with no further input than the idea itself.[34] Moreover, as more and more people exchanged ideas, a society could reach the point of a 'combinatorial explosion' whereby the interaction of ideas yielded yet further ideas at an exponential rate. Hence the modern societies that dominated the production of new ideas – rich countries with the top universities, research institutions and corporate research departments – could in principle continue to dominate indefinitely.

Needless to say, none of these theories anticipated that rich countries would ever experience an outright reversal of growth, of the sort that now seems to be happening in developed countries. To try to get a grasp on what was happening, I spoke to the colleagues I did the Covid modelling with to see if the same sort of inverse relationship between wealth and resilience we'd uncovered might be replicated in economic performance. When we modelled wealth per capita against growth, what we uncovered was a sort of law of diminishing returns: that in the earlier stages of an economy's development, wealth accumulation by the country's citizens supported growth – perhaps by providing larger pools of capital to fuel investment. But curiously, past a certain threshold, which appeared to be around the point a country passes the middle-income mark, the effect diminished and ultimately went into reverse. As countries grew richer, their economic growth rate got slower.

This raised an intriguing possibility about the peculiar phenomenon we're now witnessing of a handful of wealthy Western countries seeing their per capita incomes start to decline: in such cases, while the overall growth of the economy continues, it is more than eaten up by population growth. And that raises the question of whether the rise of wealth gradually slows growth until a point is reached that an economy can actually begin to go backwards.

Taking from the future to give to the present

We do have some instances of this happening, starting with Japan, the first developed country to enter a long stagnation and thus a case that may offer some clues as to what's going on. The country's rapid postwar economic growth drew millions of people to its cities, driving up property values until, at the peak of the boom, the land under Tokyo's Imperial Palace was worth more than all the combined real estate in California.[35] But of course, prices like this drove up the price of everything else, raising the cost of doing business and so causing Japanese cities to lose business to other, cheaper Asian destinations. Eventually, the bubble burst in 1992, and both the economy and per capita income have barely risen since.[36] Moreover, the government has run fiscal deficits far greater than the modest growth rate of the economy, which has averaged less than 1 per cent per year. In other words, it's building up a massive stock of debt, now at twice the size of annual output and rising, just to keep from going backwards – essentially, running a tab to keep the lights on.[37]

Accumulating debts, as the Japanese and US governments have done, has been one way to go backwards. But the phenomenon isn't confined to those two cases alone, nor only to governments. In other Western countries whose governments have been more tight-fisted, one consequence has been that private debt has instead taken up the slack. So, for instance, while Canada's government has maintained one of the tightest balance sheets, households and businesses have run up Japan-style debts amounting to over twice annual output.[38] By and large, when you add such private debts to public debts across Western countries, you get a ratio of debt to GDP – the total stock of a country's debt, expressed in the number of years it would take the economy to produce enough output to match it – that ranges from around three to one, in the case of the US and Britain, to as much as five to one, in Japan. These are levels of indebtedness that are unprecedented not only in the history of the West, but in all human history. The phenomenon is ubiquitous, as even the most tight-fisted of them all, Germany, doesn't do that much better at a ratio of debt to GDP of more than two to one.[39]

Germany is worth considering in this context. Its famed comparative prudence is exaggerated somewhat, since it used a technique to massage its debt figures – namely, avoiding borrowing by instead running down capital. You just have to contrast German trains of a few decades ago with those of today, which are regularly late, cancelled and frequently dilapidated, to see that Germany kept its books balanced mainly by allowing its infrastructure to degrade. (One German train conductor made himself popular when he sarcastically announced, as his train left the station, that while the bad news was none of the toilets were operating that day, the good news was neither was the restaurant car, lessening the need for them.) When the German government was finally forced to face up to the effects of all this erosion in 2025, its debt began to shoot upwards, rivalling those of other Western countries. The country has hardly been unique, though, in using this method to keep taxes and debt low. Across the West, governments have run down their capital or privatized state firms and then spent, rather than reinvested, the proceeds. In consequence, almost all Western countries have seen their net public wealth decline over the last few decades;[40] only Norway, which has invested its huge returns on oil and gas, can today guarantee its citizens a future as prosperous as its present.

There is a school of thought in economics that says none of this matters. A government that borrows in a currency it issues can borrow endlessly, since it can always print more money; moreover, printing more money needn't be a problem, since all the money it injects into the economy increases its size, the result being that it generates the revenue that will later pay its debt. As the economist Stephanie Kelton put it in her bestseller *The Deficit Myth: Modern Monetary Theory and the Birth of the People's Economy*, 'If we wanted to, we could pay off the debt immediately with a simple keystroke.'[41]

While the maths behind this Modern Monetary Theory, to which Kelton subscribes, can get a bit arcane, in truth debt is something that even some economists struggle to comprehend. That's because most of us assume that if we owe money, there must be someone else we owe it to – someone whose savings the bank has drawn upon to give us credit. But ever since the invention of fractional-reserve banking, much of the debt we incur is not borrowed from someone else, but effectively from our future selves. When you obtain a mortgage from the bank, there isn't someone else lending you money; instead, the bank creates new money, which you will repay from your future earnings. The bank does this by depositing a small percentage of the loan's value as security at the central bank, which it takes from its reserves, and then issuing a payment equivalent to the value of the loan, which the seller's bank accepts since it's all backed by the central bank. In effect, therefore, debt amounts to a means of redistributing money from your present to your future. The same is true for countries. If a government issues a bond that will be repaid only in one hundred years, it's effectively promising its lenders that the economy of the future will be sufficiently big to easily meet that payment.

Historically, it has ever been thus. Western governments have carried much bigger debt loads in the past than they do today, notably at the end of the Second World War, and paying them off has never been a problem. But those debts were incurred at a time when Western economies were growing strongly. They aren't now, and it's looking like an increasingly risky bet that they ever will again, despite the magic solutions politicians keep telling us they have up their sleeves. That's why debt-to-GDP ratios keep rising and public assets keep degrading – because growth is, if anything, going the other way.

The zamindar's tale

Running up debts and running down capital to maintain appearances is the sort of tale one associates with aristocrats falling on hard times. In his 1958 masterpiece *The Music Room*, the Indian filmmaker Satyajit Ray told the story of a feudal zamindar's decline amid a rapidly changing world. Jealous of a lower-caste neighbour who is gradually building a business empire that eclipses his own wealth, the zamindar maintains the illusion of his continued superiority by staging lavish musical events, which he funds by running up his debts and selling the family jewellery, until he finishes in ruin. As a metaphor for a Western world engaged in similar behaviour when faced with the rise of its erstwhile periphery, it seems irresistible, even though the zamindar's wealth was rooted in an agrarian economy that was dying whereas that of the West is rooted in technologies that can keep evolving.

And yet: when it comes to the value of landed property versus technology, there is one other insight from the Japanese case discussed above that is relevant to the current predicament of Western economies, and may just keep the zamindar's story current. It concerns the evolving role of asset-price bubbles. Speculative bubbles have run through the history of capitalism and held a particular fascination to some of its scholars, most notably Karl Marx and an Austrian economist who took Marx's cyclical theory of progress but ran in a more market-friendly direction, Joseph Schumpeter. To Schumpeter, bubbles and crashes were instrumental to the development of capitalism, driving a process he referred to as creative destruction. During the inflation of a bubble, money would flood into new businesses, enabling their owners to develop novel, transformative technologies. But because investors were indiscriminate, a lot of inefficient firms merely riding the wave would grow rich, until the assets became so expensive and unproductive that buyers stopped coming. At that point, the bubble would burst, asset prices would collapse, and the firms that were most efficient and actually making money would be able to pick up the clients of failing businesses and take over the sector, thereby making the economy more dynamic and efficient. Or, as Warren Buffett would later put it pithily, you found out who was skinny-dipping when the tide went out.

In contrast to these creative bubbles, though, real estate bubbles, of the sort that sank Japan and later almost crashed the world economy in 2008, create little in the way of new technologies. For its part, housing itself produces nothing. But what property bubbles do produce, when they finally burst, are a lot of angry owners who, being voters, make governments reluctant to allow creative destruction to do its stuff. Equally, because the banks have become so exposed to real estate – a very large share, sometimes over half, of their loan portfolio is used to buy real estate[42] – market crashes can threaten the stability of the financial system, making central banks equally reluctant to let them crash. The result is that what Schumpeter considered a natural process of birth, death and renewal has been interrupted, which helps to explain why the resulting bailouts and fiscal rescues get bigger and more expensive with each crisis – because the wealth that needs to be preserved keeps rising. It's thus noteworthy that the share of real estate in the wealth of Western countries has been rising over time, which would seem to herald a future of slow growth.[43] The zamindar's decline fuelled the rise of his capitalist neighbours. Were he alive today, he might have been bailed out.

A treadmill that requires us to spend more to stay rich; a gradual shift of wealth from technology to real estate; running down wealth and running up debts to keep ourselves in the standard we've come to expect; supporting asset prices and bailing out owners amid downturns, possibly at the risk of economic renewal. These relatively novel features of Western capitalism, seemingly both cause and consequence of slowing economic growth, raise an interesting thought. We saw in the last chapter how the increasing wealth of Western societies apparently caused behavioural and social changes that may have reduced societal resilience in the face of a major ecological shock. Could it equally be that increasing wealth also alters our behaviour, and that of the society as a whole, in such a way that economies become less dynamic? And might it also be that in slowing growth, behavioural and social changes put us in a paradoxical situation in which, in order to preserve our wealth, we must eat into our future income – literally, growing poorer to stay rich?

5

THE WEALTH TRAP

Anyone who's spent any length of time unwillingly unemployed can tell you that there are few things that can improve mental health more than gaining freedom from financial anxiety. Nothing vindicates the conviction that wealth is a great liberator more than the feeling you get when you go from being broke to having money in the bank and more on the way.

And yet the previous chapter raised a provocative thought: that past a certain point, wealth might turn into a sort of trap, one that forces a country to spend more to stay rich until ultimately the cost of staying rich consumes so many resources that the country's stock of wealth begins to erode. This idea parallels what we found about societal resilience to ecological shocks. In Chapter 3, we learned that as countries grow wealthier, the behaviour of their citizens changes in such a way as to raise the cost of resilience.

This chapter probes a similar possibility – that as societies grow richer, their citizens' behaviour also changes in such a way as to reduce the flexibility, adaptability and dynamism of their economy, all while raising the cost of staying rich. What's more, in the course of this process, a society advances beyond creating wealth to actually blocking its further creation. Which is to say that after a society has attained a great state of wealth, it may need to grow poorer to stay rich. This sort of unplanned degrowth resembles the flight of Icarus: when a society flies too high, it will eventually begin to fall to earth.

Let us see how this might happen.

When what you own owns you

We saw in the last chapter that rich societies are older than they were a century ago. That's not accidental, since wealth ages a society, both literally and figuratively. That in turn alters the character of the economy in profound ways.

Let's start with the literal aspect of ageing. Wealth makes a society older in that it raises the average age of the citizens via two channels, both of which have a restraining effect on growth. Firstly, as incomes rise, fertility declines. This is one of the most reliable rules of development, and while it has many drivers,[1] the basic fact is that in pre-industrial societies, children can contribute to family finances by being a source of labour, usually from a very young age. On the other hand, children in rich societies attend school and don't enter the workforce until they have attained independence from their families, acting instead as a net drain on family resources. So, the natural tendency in the latter case is to have fewer of them. Whereas a century ago in most Western societies, the average couple had around four children, today they have half that, or less.

Secondly, as incomes rise, people live longer. The average Briton lived to be sixty in 1939; today they make it past eighty. Italy's improvement was even more impressive, going from fifty-seven to eighty-three. The most dramatic of all, however, has been Japan, whose life expectancy nearly doubled from forty-eight to eighty-four in the same period. That's because nutrition improves as we can afford healthier foods – and enough of it never to go hungry – while more resources are available for healthcare. Whereas childhood and retirement once bookended human lives, today retirement has turned into an entirely new chapter in life, one that can even outlast most people's careers and has given rise to a whole industry dedicated to helping people live their best lives.

Wealthy societies therefore have fewer young people, longer retirements and pension regimes that have gone from being welfare programmes keeping people indigent in their final years to providing incomes that support them during golden years in which they maintain their standard of living. In the 1950s, the British state pension alone consumed 2 per cent of GDP;[2] today that figure has reached 5 per cent, and on its current path it will only increase, with private pensions raising that figure further.

This ageing of the population then alters the behaviour of both individuals and societies in such a way as to slow economic growth. It raises the dependency ratio, as we've seen, which increases the share of economic output committed to consumption, thereby depressing the investment share. After the war, for instance, Americans routinely set aside 10–15 per cent[3] of their income towards savings, creating a large pool of capital in the banking system; today, that figure hovers closer to 5 per cent. The fall in other countries has been even more precipitous, with Japan's saving rate going from nearly 20 per cent as late as the 1980s to about a tenth of that today.[4] Compare that to Ethiopia's savings rate of near 20 per cent,[5] India's around 30 per cent,[6] Indonesia's of nearly 40 per cent[7] or China's unrivalled rate of almost 50 per cent.[8] A 2025 study by the Organisation for Economic Co-operation and Development (OECD) found that businesses are reducing the share of revenues they allocate to investment in order to meet investor expectations of higher dividends, aligning with the need for pension funds to meet rising demands for payouts.[9]

Figuratively, wealth also ages a society in that its behaviour, notably its investment and spending behaviour, changes as it grows richer, mimicking a pattern that comes with an individual's ageing. The essence of this evolution is captured in the phrase often attributed to Winston Churchill that 'if you're not a liberal at twenty you have no heart, and if you're not a conservative at forty you have no brain'. An economist puts it differently, saying that when you have no assets, the opportunity cost of moving fast and breaking things is next to zero since the worst that can happen from a failed experiment is perhaps a setback to one's career plans, easily made up in the course of a long life ahead.

As a result of this tendency to greater caution as one ages, people become more risk-averse. Ever since Kenneth Arrow's pioneering research on decision-making in conditions of uncertainty, a rich literature on risk aversion has emerged that has generally found that as people age, they regret financial losses more than young people, probably because they feel they have less time to earn them back[10] – which helps explain why financial advisors advise clients to be more cautious as they get nearer retirement, to buy fewer of the shares that deliver them higher returns but can also incur greater losses, and more of the government bonds whose dividends may be more modest but are also more certain. This tendency towards greater risk aversion also develops as people grow richer,[11] no doubt because the more you have, the more aware you become of what you stand to lose.

People consequently grow conservative, perhaps less creative, and more inclined to preserve than to create wealth. That helps to explain why, as we saw in the last chapter, the share of real estate in the total wealth of Western societies has risen. Part of this is down to a life-cycle effect – you don't actually acquire your house until you pay off your mortgage, later in life – and part of it is the growing popularity of real estate as an investment vehicle for pension funds.[12] But part of it also reflects a rule that my grandmother used to express: 'land doesn't disappear', a legacy of the family lore about a fortune lost in a stock market swindle.

Therefore, not only does the investment share of the economy decline as wealth rises, so too does the character of investment, away from productive capital like new business ventures to non-productive capital like real estate and established, dividend-paying businesses.[13] The thing about real estate is that the income it generates can't be raised with increases in productivity, since anything other than agricultural land produces no further output. Expressed in economic terms, the value of a landed asset can't be inflated by improving its efficiency and thereby raising the margins on its output, which is to say its profits. Its value can only be increased through raising its rents, which economists define as a payment to the owner of an asset that exceeds the costs needed to produce it. So, for instance, if it costs $100,000 for someone to build a house on a piece of land next to yours, but you want to drive up the value of your own house, you can lobby the relevant authority to prevent the construction, thereby forcing your frustrated neighbour to buy your house at a higher price. Rent, in short, is generated not by raising output but by reducing it and engineering scarcity.

The rising importance of real estate in a country's wealth portfolio accordingly creates an asset-owning class that has a vested interest in limiting growth through anti-competitive behaviour, or what's known as NIMBYism ('not in my backyard'). As one institutional investor in real estate put it, housing shortages are 'supportive of cash flow'.[14] This NIMBYism, in turn, works on the labour market in a few ways that provide further headwinds to growth. First, by raising housing costs for prospective buyers or tenants – typically, young working people – it reduces fertility by raising the cost of expanding household size.[15] That reduces the long-term rate of growth in the labour force, setting the dependency ratio on a course to ever higher levels, ultimately swallowing up ever more of future output.

Second, there's also truth in the old adage that what you own owns you. One of the effects of widespread homeownership is that labour mobility declines,[16] which inhibits the efficient allocation of resources: an unemployed person might be just the right person for a job advertised elsewhere in the country, but if they are unable to sell their house, they are less likely to move than someone who can end their tenancy. John Steinbeck's classic Depression-era novel *The Grapes of Wrath* chronicled the move of an 'Okie' family that, after the Dust Bowl devastated their livelihoods, joined the 1930s exodus from America's farm belt to the ostensibly more promising fields of California. My father recounted similar tales from his early childhood, of Welsh miners standing under London street lamps singing for spare change to cover their expenses as they too joined a migration to more prosperous parts of Britain. But before the Second World War, most people in Britain and America rented their homes, whereas today most own them.[17] As a result, such mass movements are more difficult today, since selling a home in an economic downturn is especially hard precisely because the market has fallen. Instead, the strong tendency is to hang on and wait for things to turn for the better.

Third, the spread of homeownership produces an asset-owning class with a high propensity to political participation, which gives added weight to their voice. Given that property owners exhibit higher levels of political involvement than renters,[18] including not just voting but such things as attending municipal planning meetings, this locks in a tendency towards the sort of anti-growth politics that NIMBYism embodies: few want more housing to be built in their neighbourhood for fear it will depress their property values, and so they will exploit what opportunities there are – for instance, at planning meetings – to block further development. As political commentator Ezra Klein has put it, 'The people who show up to block an affordable housing complex are the people who live on that block now, not the people who *would* live on that block if the complex was built.'[19]

Finally, given that such a large share of the electorate is directly exposed to vagaries in the property market, they react strongly to falls in their asset values. That in turn gives both governments and central banks a strong incentive to rescue them with bailouts during any market crashes. Prior to the Second World War, despite frequent crashes, bank bailouts were rare;[20] since the 1970s, they have become the norm in Western countries. That further helps explain the tendency for the scale of government stimulus programmes during recessions to grow over time. With house prices underwritten they tend to rise, which means bailouts and rescues simply grow bigger, because the price falls become so much greater. (Unlike the 1929 crash, after which it took share values twenty-five years to return to their previous levels, even major crashes like that of 2008 are today largely made up within just a few years.)[21] All told, ageing societies increasingly tend to produce a politics[22] that favours the preservation of wealth rather than its creation – and the richer they are, the harder they fall, and the more that must be spent to return them to their previous level.

Go south, young man

In 2008, as the world's stock markets crashed and the global economy teetered on a cliff edge, I found myself sitting in the office of the Jamaican prime minister. I'd just created a small think tank to advise governments in the Caribbean on economic policy and so had suddenly been thrust into the rapids of a crisis. The moment was tense. Though the PM projected confidence in his public declarations, he confided to me that morning that what could be the final shipment of diesel to the island had arrived in port. With the world financial system seized up, shipping companies couldn't pay for goods or fuel, so their vessels couldn't leave the ports in which they were docked. Global shipping came to a standstill. Jamaica's electricity supply depended on imported fuel, and if shipping didn't resume soon, supplies would run out and the grid would collapse. If that happened, the banks would stop operating. Which, in turn, meant the police wouldn't be paid. The scenario led our thoughts careening downwards.

However, I told him then that amid all this gloom, there was one glimmer of hope. To jolt the financial system to life, Ben Bernanke, the chairman of the US Federal Reserve, had announced that the American central bank would not only slash interest rates to zero but would directly pump money into the economy by buying government and corporate bonds. Not long afterwards, 'Helicopter Ben' – the nickname he'd earned by once channelling Milton Friedman's suggestion that in a crisis central banks could drop money over everyone by helicopter – was soon followed by Mario Draghi, who said the European Central Bank he then ran would do 'whatever it takes' to keep the eurozone from collapsing. Other central banks followed suit, and the era of cheap and abundant money began. For the next fifteen years, these ultra-loose monetary policies would continue until finally a 2022 inflation surge made central banks pull in their horns, raising interest rates and curtailing their bond buying – though at this point governments took up the baton, launching massive spending programmes to rebuild industry, boost militaries and cut taxes.

From that 2008 vantage point in a sunlit Jamaican office, therefore, I could foresee a flood of money driving down interest rates. 'When the dust has settled,'

I told the prime minister, 'there will be loads of money in Western countries, looking for returns in an environment where interest rates are nearly zero. Investment and lending opportunities here will beckon, creating new possibilities for us.'

I pictured it like a crowd of people streaming towards a concert when they reach a pair of closed gates. The crowd builds up like an accordion and the flow eventually trickles to a stop. One of the gates then opens and everyone standing before it filters through. After a moment those standing before the closed gate drift over and join the flow. The crowd moves more slowly than it did before it reached the gates, but it is nonetheless moving again.

That metaphor may capture the effect of ageing in Western societies on the world economy. A blocked gate slows but doesn't stop the flow. Instead, it goes elsewhere. And in the modern world economy where we make our lives, that elsewhere is the developing world.

In Chapter 3, we saw how de-risking a society can make it more vulnerable to ecological shocks like the Covid-19 pandemic. It may just be that it also makes it less economically dynamic. Because the essence of capitalist dynamism is risk-taking, experimentation, innovation, discovery – all things we associate with youth. Or as Kris Kristofferson put it in his classic song 'Me and Bobby McGee', 'Freedom's just another word for nothin' left to lose'. The more you stand to lose with a risky decision, and the less you stand to gain, the less likely you are to take it.

As risk-taking declines, so does innovation, and slowing innovation has become a feature of Western societies. While globally, the rate of new patent creation has been declining in recent years,[23] China's rate has soared.[24] In contrast, the rate of new patent creation has tapered off in the United States and begun falling in Japan. Overall, the growth rates in new patents across the developing world now stand well above growth rates in Western countries.[25] Developed countries still account for a large share of innovation, given their historical accumulation of the institutional, human and financial capital that makes it possible, but the trend is clear: they are now innovating more slowly than the up-and-comers, a trend that will probably be intensified by the US administration's assault on universities and scientific research since 2025.

As innovation declines, so do improvements in human productivity. But while the rate of innovation is accelerating in developing countries, what really explains the higher productivity gains we now see there is something more prosaic, namely the application of existing technology in countries where labour and land costs remain lower. In recent decades, most of the productivity growth in the world economy has been produced in developing countries, led by Asia.[26] This reflects greater additions of capital to production. Although the whole world has seen the rate of productivity growth decline since the pandemic, the slowest growth of all lies in advanced economies, where it is now approaching zero. This fits into the picture that emerges in the aggregate data which points to a world economy whose growth is slowing, but slowing fastest of all in the rich countries. To use our previous analogy, the gate closed so everyone was flowing through the open one.

In the economy, that flow takes the form of goods, services, people and, most important of all, capital. Given the high cost of both workers and land in Western countries – and high land costs also drive up wage costs, since workers have to pay their rent – there is an obvious attraction of moving operations to the global periphery, where lower costs can produce higher returns, which in turn inflates incomes. All of the world's most expensive cities[27] are in developed countries and the most expensive cities in the developing world, like Mexico, are still markedly less expensive: Mexico has an average cost of real estate about a quarter of New York's while Jakarta's is about a twentieth. It's not that cities in the Global South are more affordable to their residents, because they can be relatively dear places to live for locals. (In proportion to the country's per capita income, for instance, Mexico is still more expensive than New York and Jakarta is more expensive than Toronto or Amsterdam.) But given that the rent paid by tenants, whether residents or business owners, plays a large part in determining the wages that must be paid or the prices businesses must charge on their products, the absolute cost of a city's property helps determine its global competitiveness. And in a world of free movement of people, goods, services and capital, that means the cost of doing business in Jakarta ends up being a good deal lower than in most major cities in the developed world.

Of course, wage and land costs are not the only things business managers consider when deciding where to locate their operations. They consider such things as proximity to suppliers and markets, security, stability of electricity and water supply, the costs of corruption or dealing with officialdom. There are many things that traditionally have raised the cost of doing business in developing countries, reducing or even eliminating any straightforward cost advantages they may have had. However, these are all areas in which developing countries have made substantial improvements in recent decades,[28] turning themselves into more receptive zones for foreign investment – India, for instance, largely abandoning the 'permit-licence raj' that inhibited business activity in the post-independence period. Oxford Economics compiles a ranking of the world's global cities,[29] and while the traditional financial capitals of the world like London and New York still dominate the list, the fastest-growing cities are those in the former global periphery – in India, the Middle East, South East Asia and West and North Africa.[30]

The backstory to what has been a recent development goes back centuries. In 1800, the time when Europe's empires were beginning the most dramatic phase of their expansion, there weren't really rich and poor countries. Across the globe, average per capita incomes stood at more or less the same level – somewhere around $1,500 in today's dollars, with Argentina and South Africa right about that level, the US and UK slightly above it and India and China slightly below it.[31] But over the next two centuries, as the European empires spread across the planet and exploited the resources, markets and labour of their colonies, their economies blossomed and one former colony, America, grew into a superpower. This was how the West ascended until it ultimately became the richest and most technologically advanced society history had ever known. At its peak, at the end of the twentieth century, the average citizen of a Western country earned about fifty times what a person in the developing world did.

However, that wage inflation reduced the international competitiveness of Western firms, not least when their former colonies in the developing world were rising fast using much cheaper labour. In the second half of the twentieth century, a massive human migration from the interiors of developing countries to the major cities along the rivers and coastlines that connected them to the global economy created vast pools of labour that, thanks to the expansion of education after decolonization, raised workers' average skill levels.

Western governments, faced with slowing economies that could not support their ageing populations, needed to find new ways to boost the revenues of the firms owned by the pension funds supporting their growing armies of pensioners. Opportunity beckoned in all those poor countries, to which were added the countries of the former Soviet bloc once the Berlin Wall fell in 1989 and they opened themselves for business. They had lots of inexpensive workers, and as the earlier technological innovations were now spreading there, their productivity was rising. Meanwhile, in the last two decades of the twentieth century, governments across the developing world, and in the former Soviet bloc states, had instituted reform programmes that reduced budget deficits, eased trade, opened capital markets and made it easier for Western companies to operate there. For their part, Western governments reasoned that capturing some of that energy would help renew their economies. So, starting in the last two decades of the twentieth century, they liberalized their own rules on the movement of capital and goods to enable their firms to 'outsource' operations to the wider world.

As a result, whereas for most of the history of the Western world the direction of capital flows in the world economy had favoured it, around the turn of the millennium that went into reverse.[32] The flow of investment towards the former periphery of the world economy then accelerated its economic growth while slowing that of the rich countries. Paradoxically, at the same time as Western economies began slowing, their wealth mushroomed. In large measure that was because outsourcing to low-wage zones raised profits by reducing costs. Profits doubled in the 1990s[33] and then tripled in the next decade, which meant wealth was growing faster than that of the economy as a whole.[34] Not only did those rising profits boost share values – the S&P500 index having risen some sixty times over,[35] for an average annual increase over 9 per cent – but the lower cost of doing business kept inflation down for decades. That enabled central banks to keep interest rates low, which kept Western economies awash with money, much of which went into property and stock markets. Whereas wealth had hitherto been the accumulated surplus of economic output, now the wealth of Western citizens – in truth, the richest tenth among them – was rising faster than that output: since the turn of the millennium, the US economy has tripled in size;[36] its net wealth, though, has quadrupled.[37]

The rich countries had reached a point where, in order to preserve their wealth, they had to eat into their own growth.

Crossing the threshold from growth to degrowth

So that raises a provocative question: could this continual slowing of growth in order to preserve wealth reach the point where growth actually turns negative? That is to say, could countries actually start growing poor to stay rich?

Economists have long known that as an economy becomes richer, its growth rate slows. This has traditionally been attributed to base effects. Expressed in mathematical terms, we'd say that as the denominator of a fraction grows larger, which is to say as the total size of the economy grows, the increment added each year, which is the numerator, will have to grow even larger than the previous year's if it is to maintain the growth rate. It is therefore to be expected that as an economy gets bigger, its growth rate will diminish until it reaches something like a steady-state expansion. That was long the expectation in the dominant neoclassical model of economic growth, as originally formulated in the

Solow-Swan model discussed in Chapter 4. But what is now happening is that after slowing for decades, the richest economies of the world, in the West, are going backwards. As already noted, in per capita terms, several Western countries are now seeing their growth rates approach zero and a couple have experienced periodic declines: Canada and the UK have done so in recent years, while at the start of 2025, France and Germany[38] saw their real per capita incomes begin to fall too.

The omens suggest more of this is coming. While the net wealth of Western countries has exploded in recent decades, the net wealth of almost all their governments has been falling, as we saw in the last chapter. One way to interpret this is as a transfer of public assets to private hands, suggesting a sort of cannibalization of the state. Equally we could interpret the accumulation of public debt, especially when not matched by an equivalent increase in public assets, as taking income from future generations – who will have to pay the debts – to sustain the position of the existing one. To this one can add the straight redistribution to preserve the wealth of asset owners, as the Trump administration did when its 2025 Big Beautiful Bill transferred money from the poorest Americans, by cutting their services, to the richest in the form of tax cuts: a society that literally started going backwards to keep its wealthy in the style to which they'd grown accustomed. All told, Western countries look to have transitioned from being productive economies to being rentier ones, where the population increasingly lives off its accumulated wealth rather than its output.

In other words, beyond a certain point, wealth appears to act as a sort of dead weight, slowing an economy and reducing its dynamism, nimbleness, vigour and resilience. The question to consider, then, is whether these slowdowns turn out to be structural and permanent or, thanks to new investment, like Germany's huge fiscal stimulus or the technological revolution that might be unleashed by AI, end up being merely cyclical.

Even if a technological miracle comes along to revive the West – and we'll see later why this might be a bit much to bank on – the headwinds to further growth look to be multiplying, even to the point they could conceivably counteract some or even all of the added productivity new technology might bring. The growth of a rentier economy may be irreversible, given that a large and political influential class has come to depend upon it. For instance, 2021 saw the most rapid growth ever in UK net wealth, with most of the increase in value being driven by land.[39] This kind of inflation in turn only strengthens the incentive for fund managers to shift capital offshore to more productive economies. And so, after the 2008 global financial crisis, the flow of investment across developed economies fell, but that towards developing economies held up[40] – a trend that, following a brief interruption at the start of the pandemic, quickly resumed.[41]

The export of capital, in turn, while preserving asset values has depressed wage growth. Since the 1980s, the ratio of wages to profits has trended downwards, with profits rising faster than wages.[42] All this, as we've seen, has depressed fertility, with the native-born population now falling in several Western societies – Japan, Greece, Hungary, South Korea and Canada among them.

A falling population, not least one that is ageing and thus exiting the productive economy, all but guarantees future economic decline. In consequence, Western countries have increasingly had to resort to immigration to maintain their labour forces. This, however, has provoked a backlash. Right-wing populist parties, which have made opposition to immigration a central element of their platform, have risen in importance alongside the increase in immigration. Support for this new anti-immigrant movement appears to come from two principal groups in society: older voters who resent the rapid cultural change the increasing diversity of the society has caused, and economically active voters – not just workers but small business people – who feel economically threatened by immigration.[43] Across the West, anti-immigrant parties have both grown their support while also pushing mainstream parties further to the right on immigration, to the point that even a

Social Democratic premier like Denmark's, or a Labour Home Secretary in Britain, can espouse anti-immigrant politics. Although not many countries are going so far as to deploy armed brigades like the United States' Immigration and Customs Enforcement (ICE) who are hunting down immigrants the administration considers undesirable, virtually all are clamping down on immigration. Even famously immigrant-friendly Canada has begun to substantially reduce the number of immigrants it says it will accept each year.[44]

It appears, therefore, that economic growth ultimately produces political feedback loops that further inhibit economic growth. This raises an interesting thought. In Chapter 3, we saw how wealth reduced societal resilience and raised its cost amid the shock of the Covid crisis, the result being that in relative terms, wealthier countries were hit harder and had to spend more to make it through the pandemic than poor ones did. What this chapter reveals is that wealth has also inhibited the rebound of rich countries from the economic shock of the pandemic. That helps explain why developing countries bounced back from the recession more quickly than rich ones did, despite the latter having supposedly enjoyed more propitious conditions.

Taken together, these two discoveries raise an intriguing possibility. As we'll go on to see in the next chapter, economic growth is producing ecological feedback loops that are impeding further growth, and while Covid-19 was the first major such shock, it will all but certainly not be the last. Not only does the continued encroachment of agriculture into hitherto forest regions ensure there will be more zoonotic disease outbreaks, to which one can add the development of antibiotic-resistant superbugs, but climate change is expected to wreak havoc on economies. Until now, the dominant assumption in the discussion of the economics of climate change has been that while rich countries caused the problem with their carbon-intensive rapid growth, poor countries will bear much of the cost since they are on the front lines of climate change – more of them being located close to the equator where temperature rises will be felt most acutely – while they also lack the resources needed to adapt to change.

Instead, we may now face a novel possibility: that just as they did with their economic recovery from the pandemic, developing countries may be better placed to recover from the economic shocks of climate change than rich ones, and that it will thus be rich countries that end up feeling the consequences of their past behaviour.

6

THE KILL SWITCH WITHIN

We have long known that there are ecological feedback loops that result from rapid economic development, from species change and extinction to climate change and desertification. The Gaia hypothesis tried to integrate these into a synthesis which postulated that nature puts limits on human activity. But what the last chapter revealed is that the biggest natural limit to economic growth may come not from the external environment but from the internal one – from within ourselves, our own nature, and how that seems to make us change as we grow richer. This Icarus effect – that the higher we rise, the more we risk falling – seems to operate internally.

Nevertheless, the external feedback loops persist and appear to be increasing in both frequency and severity. The discussion of the previous three chapters thus sets the scene for a provocative thought: if economic growth reduces the resilience and economic dynamism of a society, and with that its ability to bounce back from the exogenous shocks that result from feedback loops like the Covid-19 pandemic and its hit to economic output, does it also mean that rich countries will be more vulnerable to the feedback loops related to climate change? As these shocks multiply, will rich countries be less able to absorb and respond to the likes of regular floods, droughts, wildfires and heatwaves than they imagine? Is the fact that the developed economies are flying higher than everyone else the very thing that makes them, like Icarus as he approached the sun, the most vulnerable?

Karma might be a bitch after all

To the conventional wisdom, the suggestion that rich countries will suffer the most damage from climate change would be not only bold, but even preposterous. As we learned in Chapter 2, the literature on the economics of climate change has long been clear: although rich countries did most of the damage, poor countries will pay the lion's share of the price. As the head of the climate fund created by the Paris Agreement put it, 'climate is going to jeopardise development and it's going to exacerbate inequality in the world' by driving poor countries relatively further behind rich ones.[1]

The first point, that Western countries produced most of the carbon emissions that triggered climate change, now lies beyond reasonable contestation. Western defenders of the status quo will sometimes say that while Western economies are decarbonizing – per capita greenhouse gas emissions are now declining in most Western countries[2] – they are rising rapidly in the developing world; and since these emissions are what will push the planet past the perceived tipping point of 1.5 degrees of warming, it is developing countries that must adjust their development strategies and do what rich countries are now doing, which is to invest heavily in decarbonization.

However, framing the discussion this way amounts to tipping the scales, because it only counts future emissions and not past ones. The numbers are broadly incontestable on this. Scientists estimate that since the dawn of humanity, the amount of carbon dioxide that the earth's atmosphere could absorb without warming more than 1.5 degrees – the figure that has been set as the tipping point beyond which the damage done by climate change begins to seriously challenge human societies – has been about 3,000 billion tons.[3] If we then take that figure and divide it by the total number of humans who've ever lived – maybe 100 billion[4] – we'd each get a lifetime personal allocation of 30 tons. For most of our history as a species, no individual ever came near to using that lifetime allowance. But around 1850, after fifty thousand years in which our ancestors lived within their carbon budgets, the residents of the Western world began to heavily outspend their carbon credits. In the relatively short time since then, a handful of Western countries burned through more than four-fifths of the total planetary allowance,[5] with most of that having been consumed just since the middle of the last century. The economic golden age that followed the Second World War didn't come for free.

In effect, we in the West not only used up all the unused quotas of all previous generations, we then used up the allowance of *everyone* living today in the developing world. When even that wasn't enough, we began dipping into the allowances of future generations, much as we are with the debts we're running up to sustain our lifestyles. The average Canadian, for instance, today burns through his or her lifetime quota in about two years.[6] It's not for nothing that the world's Greta Thunbergs say the older generation stole their future.

In a moral sense, then, the right thing to do would be for the citizens of the West to pay for all the allowances they ever used, allowing developing countries to continue their development. This, in a nutshell, is the argument made by advocates of degrowth: the rich must go backwards to allow the poor to catch up. Jason Hickel argues that this reversal needn't be experienced as a setback for all but a small minority of people, since income is highly unequally spread and so results in inefficiency – for instance, Portugal has better social outcomes (such as life expectancy) than the US despite roughly half the income.[7] Unfortunately, almost all of that small minority who will experience the reversal live in Western countries, where they comprise a majority of the population, and few of them may spend much if any time contemplating what debt they might owe the rest of the world for their wealth. Despite some progress and a slew of international agreements, humanity is still advancing ever closer to a point of no return, and it's doing so because what matters to the political debate isn't the morality of Western riches but the calculus of climate change. Namely, that while all countries face unique cost–benefit calculations in determining whether to prioritize economic growth or tackle climate change, all of those calculations lead to the same outcome: no country, rich or poor, stands to gain from arresting climate change.

Let's look first at the calculus for rich countries. Assuming developed countries will be better placed to deal with climate change, the opportunity cost of stopping it exceeds the returns that will accrue to them. Most economists who have looked at the economic impact of climate change have applied scientific estimates of expected future warming on a country-by-country basis, estimating the productivity impacts of rising temperatures on each. One consequence of this approach has been that since countries closer to the equator start with higher average temperatures, they face a bleaker future than those at higher latitudes. And given that due to the accidents of fate – namely, the rise of Europe's empires and their domination of much of the world during their imperial eras – rich countries tend to be clustered in the cooler northern hemisphere whereas those closer to the equator tend to be comparatively poor, we get the pernicious rule that the poor countries that did the least to cause climate change would suffer most from its effects, whereas the rich countries that did most to cause it would suffer least.

Second, the costs of mitigating and adapting to climate change, such as installing air conditioning, building flood defences or solidifying foundations, is going to lie beyond the current means of most poor countries, whereas in rich ones it, if anything, creates business opportunities. In short, the main message to poor countries from earlier research was that nobody said life was fair. The upshot of this earlier scholarship was therefore that rich countries could afford to stand by and wait for climate change to overwhelm poor countries, which would then either be forced to decarbonize their economies, or just go under – in some cases, such as some South Pacific island nations, quite literally – the resulting impoverishment being sufficient to bring their carbon emissions back down.

Turning to look next at the poor countries, sadly, the same calculus shows they will also not decarbonize, at least not soon enough to prevent a potentially catastrophic overheating of the planet. Their reasons for not doing so differ from those of rich countries, but the outcome is the same. For them, given a choice between poverty in a sustainable world today and riches tomorrow, even the risk of future climate collapse doesn't surpass the immediate risk of poverty-related deaths from hunger or disease. After all, that amounts to no more than a choice between poverty and premature death today, and death tomorrow. Inevitably, therefore, developing countries are continuing on the road to rapid growth using carbon-intensive strategies, particularly in coal-producing countries like India, China and Indonesia. Their message to Western governments is that if they want them to decarbonize, they'll have to pay for it. Since that won't happen, we're stuck in a doom loop of continued global warming, climate change and possible ecological and even civilizational collapse one day. That, we're told, is in our nature.

But what if the basic assumptions informing this calculus are wrong? What if the cost of climate change will in fact hit Western countries hardest and knock them backwards? What if, moreover, it's doing that already? What if the foretold growth that will supposedly enable Western countries to mitigate the future effects of climate change stops, thus giving them a strong interest in dealing with it now before they go too far backwards?

From black swan to green swan

If there's been one key insight from this book so far, it's that wealth not only provides resources and strength, it also creates vulnerabilities and costs. Let's start this part of the discussion with a simple analogy, namely buying or building a house, which, as we've seen, has become a popular form of wealth accumulation in Western countries. Once you buy a house, your stock of wealth ideally surpasses what you previously had as a renter: as we all like to say, you're now paying yourself and not a landlord. On the other hand, you now incur a new set of expenses as well, from taxes and maintenance to upgrades and redecoration. Being rich, as we saw, can get expensive. And if a flood or storm comes along to damage or even destroy your house, your wealth has been reduced and possibly even destroyed. In contrast, had you still been a tenant you could have found a new home to rent.

That analogy will come in handy as we consider the recent scholarship on the economics of climate change. As we saw in Chapter 2, early writing on the topic estimated that, assuming the warming of the planet was kept to within 1.5 degrees, climate change might end up shaving some 1–3 per cent off future global economic output, with the damage falling disproportionately on the poorer countries closer to the equator. Today, we need to look at those figures in a new light. We are now closing in on the 1.5 degree threshold – in fact, by some measures, we may already have reached it and in 2023 we even briefly surpassed it, an omen of what's coming. While that year's increase was in part due to temporary factors, it is nonetheless becoming clear that the long-term average temperature is moving perilously close to the tipping point, while carbon emissions keep rising to make even the 1.5 degree target look increasingly Pollyannaish.[8]

However, what is most telling of all is that the current research on climate change is starting to challenge the relatively optimistic assessments of the earlier generation. None of the initial models anticipated a shock like the global pandemic, the attendant fall in economic output, and a subsequent resumption of growth that would turn out to be slower than before. They tended also to employ country-by-country estimates on the impact of global warming rather than looking at how changes in other countries would then rebound on countries notionally sheltered from climate change's effects, a method that produces quite different results.[9] Similarly, not all modellers have consulted extensively with their peers in relevant scientific fields and so they've often struggled to integrate concepts from the natural sciences, such as tipping points, which can completely upend forecasts;[10] in fact, those economists who have begun working tipping points into their models lean towards the view that most forecasts of the economic damages of climate change are probably underestimates.[11] All in all, a consensus now appears to be emerging among economists studying climate change's effects that the early estimates of the economic harm due to climate change, in the order of 1–3 per cent being wiped off the future global economy, were probably too low. More recent studies suggest that as much as 10–50 per cent of future output will be wiped off the world economy by climate change,[12] one influential paper going so far as to estimate that had there been no global warming since 1960, the world economy would already be 37 per cent bigger than it is today, and that the future cost of neglecting to address it will end up feeling like the equivalent of fighting a domestic war, forever.[13]

Still, even if there's widespread agreement that the cost of mitigating climate change today will be less than adapting to it later[14] – assuming the world economy continues to grow at current rates – even setbacks on this scale would not lead to global degrowth. So, someone wanting to make a case for complacency could still argue that the risk of inaction is one that we will be able to afford even in a worst-case scenario. Except that we are also getting a more nuanced picture of the economic harms of climate change, which make such risks look greater and more urgent in rich countries than was previously thought. Given that the growth of Western economies is now close to zero, and if in fact those already weak rates of growth continue slowing, setbacks of this magnitude could conceivably send several rich countries backwards, making their citizens materially poorer. In fact, it's even possible this reversal has already begun. In 2023, a summer of wildfires across Canada made it impossible for people to work for a time in agriculture, forestry and mining in affected regions while rail transportation through affected areas had to be suspended, hindering economic activity. As smoke forced people across large swathes of the country to stay indoors, there ensued an economic contraction[15] sufficient to knock the country's per capita income back 1.3 per cent that year.[16] Canada's economy was already vulnerable, and this climate shock pushed it over the edge to contraction.

In addition, many contracts and prices on such things as pension funds and real estate are today based on financial assumptions presuming higher rates of future growth than might now materialise. Most importantly of all, in contrast to earlier assumptions, more recent scholarship suggests that the earlier belief in Western countries being largely spared the economic harm of climate change now seems doubtful. Our study of the pandemic experience and subsequent economic recovery, or lack thereof, helps us understand why. Part of the reason earlier models were somewhat sanguine about the economic impacts of climate change is that, still being speculative, they had less data to work with. But what's becoming apparent today is that rather than a generalized warming of the planet that would produce localized if manageable changes to weather patterns, what's emerging are a set of feedback loops that are turning out to be more severe than originally expected.

For example, the fact that 'nobody' foresaw a shock like the pandemic coming was a failure of politics, not science. Epidemiologists had been warning since the late twentieth century that something like it would probably come along one day. In a chillingly prophetic 1996 report, the US National Institutes of Health had warned that 'Surveillance of the unknown appears to be a thankless task, and it is probable that we will learn of an "Andromeda" event after an urban population is struck, although the agent is most likely to arise in a rural, tropical setting. The health and safety of future generations may depend on our ability to rapidly detect, monitor, and control disease caused by novel zoonotic agents.'[17]

They could see what was coming because as incomes rose across the world and humanity's food appetite grew more ravenous and sought more meat, agriculture became more industrialized and pushed deeper into forest zones in regions of Asia and Africa that had previously been little exposed to the outside world, their human residents seldom venturing far outside them. The result has been the release of pathogens into widespread human circulation, producing a rise in zoonotic disease outbreaks.[18] It would therefore be irresponsible for us to think of Covid-19 as a one-off, though few if any economic forecasts allow for such shocks.

Economic forecasts, like those done in the early climate change models, don't factor in such dramatic events because they are by their nature unforeseeable, falling into the category of what Nassim Nicholas Taleb has called a 'black swan' event. In his 2007 book of the same name, Taleb used the case of the black swan as a metaphor for a highly improbable event whose impact could be huge.[19] Until they encountered black swans in Australia a couple of centuries ago, Europeans assumed all swans were white because the only swans they'd ever observed were white. Covid-19 fell into this same category. Warned by epidemiologists that such an event would come along some day, British authorities used the experience they had – of flu pandemics – to prepare contingency plans, which helped explain why the British government initially was sanguine about the risks.[20] By the time they realized they were dealing with a very different kind of outbreak, it had already spun out of control.

Taleb – whose book fatefully appeared on the eve of the global financial crisis – argued that the predictive models used by financial houses to anticipate economic shocks, like those used by the British government in the early stages of the pandemic, rely on past experience and so fail to anticipate new shocks. But now that it's becoming apparent that these feedback loops are producing effects more frequently and with more severity than previously anticipated, it seems prudent to begin erring on the side of caution and assume that such Covid-scale shocks are going to recur. We have to anticipate more black swans.

Unfortunately, pandemics aren't the only type. Among the feedback loops that could produce such black swan events are:

- The shift to monocrop production that accompanies the industrialization of agriculture, reducing seed diversity while also increasing vulnerability to a mass crop failure.

- The shift to a meat-based diet that rising incomes bring about and that is more resource-intensive and increases greenhouse gas emissions.

- An increase in the number and severity of climate change-induced extreme weather events, like droughts, floods and superstorms, along with wildfires.

- The rising cost of food production, which could permanently raise inflation and thus create financial risks.

- The migration of fungal infections[21] from tropical to northern regions due to warming temperatures, thus exposing them to populations that have built no natural resistance to them (rather as has happened with zoonotic disease outbreaks like HIV, SARS and Covid-19 itself).

- The development and spread of antibiotic-resistant superbugs due to the overuse of antibiotics across the world, itself a consequence of increased prosperity.[22]

Of these, the one feedback loop that we are clearly seeing with increased regularity and that therefore can no longer be treated as a black swan event is extreme weather. Some research is beginning to argue that, given the damage that we can now start to quantify and model, we should begin preparing for a 'green swan' event at some point in the future, one that could trigger a major global financial crisis. In a 2020 paper, the Bank for International Settlements argued that 'Traditional backward-looking risk assessments and existing climate-economic models cannot anticipate accurately enough the form that climate-related risks will take.'[23] Rather as the 2008 global financial crisis began when a wave of falling real estate prices led banks to sell assets to cover losses, launching a self-reinforcing downward spiral, analysts foresee a scenario in which an extreme weather event might cause enough losses to trigger a similar chain reaction. So far, markets and politicians have remained calm about this risk, perhaps judging there to be few rewards from preparing for something that may or may not happen on their watch.

But this sort of complacency resembles what preceded the Covid-19 pandemic. Scientists had been warning political and business leaders for decades that a major disease outbreak was due, but the threat received little attention until it hit. We all know how well that worked out.

The bigger they are, the harder they fall

The Covid-19 pandemic had been preceded by a string of zoonotic disease outbreaks that had been prevented from becoming pandemics, no doubt giving political leaders the confidence that they could manage every risk that came along – until one day they couldn't. By the same token, we might today read into the increase of climate change-induced crises a warning of shocks that, while perhaps manageable today, could eventually overwhelm our defences, because their number and severity are increasing. Take extreme weather. Since the 1960s, the average annual number of such events has risen sevenfold,[24] and in the last few years they've begun to extract an unprecedented toll: of the ten costliest extreme weather events on record in the US, six occurred in the last decade.[25] In Europe, it was seven.[26] In Canada, of the ten most costly years insurance companies have ever had to bear, nine have taken place since 2011.[27] There is no reason to believe this trend will not continue, and intensify, steadily ratcheting up these costs.

The mistaken prediction that the pandemic would hit poor countries worst and hinder their economic recoveries most was derived from a false inference: namely, that everyone would face the same shock, but greater access to resources would cushion its blow in rich countries. As we've seen, however, this assumption assigns great weight to the role of resources in resilience and underestimates the degree to which other factors affected both individual and societal resilience. And as has now been established, when it comes to the effects of extreme weather, being rich actually creates vulnerabilities. Thus, even if the impacts of climate change fall most heavily on the people that didn't cause it,[28] with flooding and diseases like malaria and cholera hitting developing countries the worst, it's now clear that the economic costs of these events are falling most heavily on rich countries, simply because there is so much more capital to be destroyed by extreme weather.[29] As the saying goes, the bigger they are, the harder they fall.

For instance, in 2023, four-fifths of the economic damage due to extreme weather occurred in developed countries, a proportion substantially higher than their share of global output.[30] This brings us back to our analogy of the costs one incurs when buying a house: one of the ways extreme weather is hitting ordinary people in developed economies is by raising the number of home repossessions resulting from damage costs, declining home values and rising insurance premiums that result from exposure to extreme weather.[31] Many houses exposed to climate risks, like storms and rising sea levels, will become uninsurable,[32] or will remain insurable only if expensive mitigation investments are made.[33] And as the number and severity of these events rises, yet more homes will be exposed.

That in turn will knock down the resale value of those properties. Given the relative illiquidity of house markets – unlike share markets, where stocks are sold and bought instantly, houses can stay on the market for months and owners unhappy with price offers will often just hold out for a better day – it takes a while for the effects of extreme weather damage to show up in average house prices. So to date, the increased severity of extreme weather hasn't profoundly changed the value of real estate. Nevertheless, Ben Keys, an expert on the financial risks of climate change at the University of Pennsylvania's Wharton School, points out that we're getting early indications of what's coming in insurance and reinsurance markets in the US, where real rates rose by as much as 20 per cent in the four years up to 2025 and municipal bond markets have begun to show early signs of strain.[34] Similarly in Europe,[35] the cost of insurance has risen faster than inflation due to the effects of extreme weather, but the amount of coverage offered by insurers has been dropping to compensate for the increased costs they are having to bear in payouts. That only raises the risk of a major shock to the financial system in the event of a climate disaster.

Among other unforeseen problems, much of the existing infrastructure and housing stock in the developed world was built with little if any expectation of the sort of extreme weather we're now seeing. For instance, most North American buildings presume the availability of air conditioning and so have limited airflow, making them ill-prepared for the expected increased frequency of power outages due to extreme weather events, which can thus aggravate the impact of heatwaves.[36] For that reason, there's a growing anxiety about the future threat of 'compound climate events'[37] – when, for instance, a heatwave causes a power failure. American cities like Phoenix, where virtually every residence is air-conditioned, would be at risk because much of the housing stock is not built to accommodate airflow and they have few contingency plans, like cooling centres, to deal with such an eventuality. In Southern Europe, in contrast, where residential air conditioning is less common, people have long done such things as taking shelter in cool, airy churches during heatwaves, while buildings are designed to release heat – for instance, with outdoor-opening shutters rather than interior curtains for shade – and maximize natural airflow.

Similarly, rail infrastructure in much of Europe isn't prepared for the extreme temperatures and weather patterns we're now starting to see, complicating travel schedules and raising maintenance costs, with one study estimating that the annual damages caused by extreme weather could rise as much as tenfold by the end of the century.[38] In addition to the negative productivity impacts of such events, re-engineering and repair will raise future maintenance costs. As these are factored into both asset prices and insurance models, the likely hit to wealth will have negative knock-on effects on the remainder of the economy.

Over time, such developments will begin to filter through to asset markets as properties gradually come on to the market, both in house prices and house-backed securities, like real estate investment trusts, along with infrastructure funds. That points to a channel of risk that a growing number of experts worry could eventually trigger a financial crisis – namely, that given the degree of exposure of the banking system to the real estate market, a fall in asset prices could eventually force banks to sell other assets to improve their liquidity, triggering a run. The risk of a future climate crash, a financial crisis triggered by a domino effect on asset values from uninsurable properties or from the (unpriced) costs of mitigation and adaptation for existing businesses,[39] is beginning to get serious attention. What would potentially make such an event more devastating than previous crashes is that it would be structural rather than cyclical. Previous crashes were caused by bubbles that burst, after which markets found a new equilibrium; but for as long as climate change keeps worsening, the pressures on markets will only build and equilibria will presumably keep moving downwards.

Compounding both growing risk in the financial system and headwinds to rising asset prices is a possible permanent increase in the rate of price inflation, due to the rising cost of food production.[40] While adaptation can mitigate some of the risks posed to agriculture by climate change, and in particular its direct exposure to extreme weather, it can't mitigate all of it.[41] We're already starting to see such price pressures: Europe's 2022 heatwaves were found to have increased price inflation from 0.4 per cent to 0.9 per cent,[42] and some models predict that an increase to headline inflation of that order, or even more, may become permanent.[43] Given that Western central banks currently target an annual inflation rate of 2 per cent, that kind of permanent upward shift will either erode living standards over time or force a permanent increase in interest rates – which in turn could reduce incomes.

Given that we're still only in the early stages of climate change and that the current path of carbon emissions heralds further worsening, we have to assume the direction of travel is going one way for now – towards decline. In other words, what we're dealing with today will not get better, and barring an abrupt change in the direction of emissions it will probably get worse. Such effects have yet to be priced into asset markets in any significant way, but it seems only a matter of time before they are.

Nature's last laugh

It's difficult to say just how much, if any, of the slowdown in Western economies is due to climate change, given the challenges of disaggregating economies and the weight of cyclical factors that can temporarily overwhelm structural ones. For instance, despite adverse effects on some of its property prices, Florida has remained a good place to invest in real estate,[44] because such short-term factors as the wave of retiring baby boomers moving to the state, the Covid boom and loose federal fiscal policy have obscured any long-term effects from climate change.[45] Nevertheless, these factors will run their course, while the long-term average rate of growth may trend downwards. That will keep the good years from being as good as they could be and make the bad years even worse.

How will these effects manifest themselves in the poorer countries of the world? While it's true that rich countries have more capital to deplete, poor countries have more people, with more than four-fifths of humanity living in developing countries, where population growth rates are usually higher, particularly in Africa. Moreover, living as so many of them do in precarious conditions, it stands to reason that though climate change is hitting rich countries harder than we expected from an economic standpoint, from a human standpoint, it should still be the citizens of poor countries who suffer the most. So, it's somewhat surprising that, so far at least, most deaths due to extreme weather have occurred in developed countries, with heatwaves in Europe proving particularly deadly.[46] The clue to resolving this enigma may lie in some research on agricultural resilience amid climate change. One study[47] has found that, with the exception of the very poorest countries — due to their dependence on cassava as a staple, which it's expected will be quite negatively affected by climate change — rich countries stand to lose the most agricultural income because hot regions are already more advanced in climate adaptation.[48]

In other words, it may be that, as happened with the pandemic, previous experience of dealing with adversity better prepares a people for dealing with it in the future. And given their long exposure to heatwaves and extreme weather, from hurricanes to monsoon flooding, people in tropical countries have developed coping mechanisms in the face of such challenges. During my childhood in Canada, a country known for its cold winters but which can also produce punishing summer heatwaves, everyone tailored their behaviour in the seasonal scorchers: drinking more water, eating more fruits and vegetables, sitting outside in the shade until late in the evening, going swimming and taking cold showers or baths before bed. Above all, everyone slowed down, turning summer into a time of languor. So, when as an adult I moved to the tropics, where I would subsequently spend the better part of my adult life, I found it quite straightforward to adapt to a place where life unfolded on verandahs, houses were built to allow airflow and the workday was tailored around the weather, with early starts and long midday breaks.

There's a large body of literature on how keeping workplace air temperatures in a moderate range improves productivity, which speaks to the effectiveness of air conditioning. But less research has been done on the impact on society of residential air conditioning,[49] which happens to have become ubiquitous in Canada since I left. Whereas Canadians once tailored their summer behaviour to the heat, and life was spent largely outdoors, today they typically spend a good deal of the summer indoors, having acclimatized to the cooler interior temperatures they now maintain. What we know of heatwaves is that in cities where residential air conditioning is less widespread, human bodies experience a more gradual adjustment,[50] which can reduce the dangers of the heat. It may therefore be that while working in climate-controlled environments improves productivity, living in them reduces resilience amid climate shocks.

In other words, it's possible that the leap required to adapt to a world of more extreme weather is one the citizens of the developing world will be able to manage more readily, even if their absolute exposure is worse. The same can probably be said for their infrastructure. Precisely because both their housing stock and infrastructure is less developed, the bulk of future construction lies ahead, which will enable them to better plan for a more volatile world. Over the long run, this may give them further cost advantages, of the sort that are making them magnets for Western investment.

Politicians in Western countries can still be heard saying we can't afford the costs of decarbonizing the economy, a pitch that lands well with voters who would rather worry about tomorrow when it comes – not to mention those old enough to reckon they won't have to deal with *that* tomorrow at all. 'Net Zero lunacy is hiking your bills & killing UK industry,' claims the Reform UK party leader Nigel Farage in a manner common to right-wing populists, making statements with little basis in reality but that effectively speak to the pocketbook concerns of voters.[51] Britain's deindustrialization happened long ago, in the coal era, and its net zero sector is now one of the economy's fastest-growing sectors.[52] Nevertheless, it's looking increasingly like the cost of climate change adaptation is no longer a distant prospect. With the frequency and the intensity of capital-destroying extreme weather events likely only to rise, the bill will keep rising in step with it – one for which we all pay the price.

Some might have once imagined that the imperative to decarbonize the world economy was a game of chicken in which Western countries, better able to adapt and more sheltered from the effects of climate change, could outlast the rising countries of the former global periphery. If so, not only is this a game of chicken that nobody wins, but in contrast to earlier expectations, it may be the West that goes over the cliff first.

This flies in the face of the modern tale, in which those who had managed to distance themselves most from nature, the rich, had emancipated themselves from its tyranny whereas those closest to it, the poor of the developing world, would be thwarted by it. But we may in fact be seeing the reverse happening, which would be quite a surprising finding.

Or not. As the next chapter argues, perhaps it's what we should have expected all along.

7

THE ICARUS ECONOMY

This book has told the story of modernity as a tale of human emancipation from nature – the ability to transcend its limits and soar to wherever the imagination might choose. Economic theory lies at the heart of this narrative. Although they imagine themselves as scientists, economists remain in essence what they were at the eighteenth-century birth of their discipline: moral philosophers, very often drawn to the discipline not because they want merely to study and understand the world, but to change it for the better. For them, the great achievement of the last few centuries' phenomenal economic growth has not merely been to make people richer – although that is certainly a plus – but to allow them more of the benefits of progress. To us, this looks like better healthcare and nutrition and hence longer, more meaningful lives; better public services, like law, order, cleaner neighbourhoods and safer streets, which allow all of us to feel more free; better schools, to allow us to fulfil more of our potential; better entertainment, and so forth.

Economists don't generally conceive our advance in a purely linear manner in which more is always more. The trajectory of human ascent is not perpendicular. The concepts of marginal utility and declining returns allow that, as humans grow richer and live longer, the rate of progress slows and the benefits of each increment of utility declines. But while the arc of progress thus gradually bends downwards, it never reverses, and in principle humans can continue rising forever, if more slowly than before. Since this is an unending process, economists seldom ponder what utopia would resemble, though one popular economics blogger, Noah Smith, imagined it as what he calls a 'shallower' existence: shallow in that, for instance, the sort of tragedies that produce great art, or heroism, or adventure, would disappear. While we might miss the art and heroism and adventure, we'd gain from the end of tragedy and loss, and thus be free to enjoy everything life offers without anxiety, pain or sorrow.

But what this book's discussion has revealed is that the story of economic progress may follow a different narrative arc, one that more accurately resembles the flight of Icarus – and that, like Icarus, the human ascent is eventually reversed because, in effect, nature calls it back. That economic growth triggers feedback loops in both the external natural environment and the internal one, which is to say within ourselves, which together slow and ultimately reverse economic growth.

This confounds the predictions of mainstream economic theory. Sclerotic growth has previously been viewed as an obstacle that new technology can overcome, as it always did in the past, and so mainstream economic theory proposes to solve the problem with measures that would accelerate technological change and induce a new economic takeoff. Faced with the sort of slowdown the West has been experiencing since the pandemic, the prescription is to do everything possible to sweep aside the obstacles to further growth.

After the post-pandemic slowdown, governments began trying ambitious programmes to do just that – consider Germany's 2025 massive infrastructure and defence spending plan, the US's Big Beautiful Bill of tax cuts in the same year, Britain's industrial policy and planning reform proposed by the Labour government after its 2024 election victory – all while exploring ways to deregulate their economies and make it easier to do business. In addition to these measures, what gives economists hope that this slowdown shall pass is their belief that human ingenuity and technology will save the day, as it has in the past.

The obvious candidate for the technology that will launch the next transformation of human capacities is artificial intelligence. The roaring rally of the 'Magnificent Seven' tech stocks in 2024–25, when the share values of seven American companies in the vanguard of AI rose so high that, together, they became more valuable than any other stock market on the planet, suggested investors fully shared that faith. If they're right and these huge bets pay off, hindsight may reveal that the period after 2008, when economies slowed across most of the developed world, was nothing more than a pause for breath between major technological breakthroughs. After the brief productivity boom in the late 1990s, which was attributed to the Internet revolution but so far looks to have been something of a false dawn, the big one may now have finally come.

Some economists go further and say we may already be in the midst of the next industrial revolution, and that the only reason it hasn't yet shown up in the data is that we're measuring the wrong things. For instance, we now spend much of our lives on social media, a good deal of which we do essentially for free. That we choose to spend so much time there suggests we derive some utility from it; but if we're paying nothing for it, that surely amounts to a highly productive technology. Erik Brynjolfsson has thus led other economists in experimenting with survey techniques that ask people the price they'd demand to renounce social media altogether, then compare it to the price they pay to actually use it – in the form of subscription fees or the advertising revenue they generate.[1] The difference between those two figures, they say, is unmeasured output. Once you add that to existing output, you would get a truer picture of how productive the economy really is, because this particular technology is producing more value than it yields in revenue.

Other economists note a sharp uptick in US labour productivity around 2023, which would seem to align with the start of the big wave of investment in AI – ChatGPT was launched at the end of 2022 – and suggests a major boom may already have begun. Certainly, the anecdotes one hears from within the AI sector, and among some employers that are using it, is that AI is making workers more productive and even replacing humans in many roles, thereby making the remaining workers more productive. (This is because productivity is measured by dividing output by the number of work hours, so reducing the latter but not the former raises productivity.)

Yet another possibility is that this recent uptick in productivity may actually reflect an earlier innovation, probably the Internet. It's often pointed out that it took some forty years before the invention of electricity produced a productivity boost, because the technology only became potent when it became sufficiently widespread to create network effects. Converting a factory to electricity made little sense if you had to produce it yourself, very expensively; but once public utilities created large supplies at low cost, and everyone was connected to the network, the cost of switching paid for itself. So, it may be that only today, some thirty-plus years since the start of the Internet revolution, its effects are starting to show up in the productivity data now that ever more of humanity is directly networked via their smartphones.

If the keepers of this faith are correct, we may therefore already have begun the next chapter of the modern tale of human triumph.

What has been will be again

Then again, maybe we haven't.

Four decades ago, the Nobel economist Robert Solow famously quipped, 'You can see the computer age everywhere but in the productivity statistics.'[2] We've been promised the next industrial revolution several times, but we're still waiting for it to begin. Nobody doubts that new technologies keep radically transforming our lives, but since Solow made that declaration, the evidence that they will also radically transform human productivity has yet to emerge for anything longer than brief periods.

Let's start with the arguments made above for the next industrial revolution. While accounting for output that isn't fully priced helps us to develop a more granular understanding of our economy, and is thus useful in its own right, the same might also have been true of the economy at any of its earlier stages of output. The satisfaction one person gains from sitting on their smartphone may or may not be superior to what an earlier generation gained from sitting on their verandah talking with neighbours, but since we didn't measure the earlier unpriced utility, we can't form a clear picture of just how much more productive – or not – the economy is today. We must consequently compare like with like, and the long-term trend in productivity growth in Western countries remains, for the most part, downwards.

Besides, although the assumption that the subjective price one attaches to an item provides an accurate indication of its utility is uncontroversial to most economists, not everyone shares that view. After all, any drug addict would attach a very high price to their drug, but concluding that this indicates the utility of the drug, as opposed merely to its market price, is problematic.[3] One experiment with Facebook users found that even though they attached a monetary value to the platform, when their access to it was limited, they reported lower depression and more engagement in healthier activities.[4] Given the growing body of research on the societal problems of social media, from mental health crises in young people to the spread of anti-democratic conspiracy theories, any measurement that fails to cost these also would be biasing itself towards a necessarily favourable conclusion.

As for the pandemic-era surge in labour productivity in the US, there have been brief bursts of productivity growth that quickly petered out – indeed the 1990s surge attributed to Internet adoption fits that bill – but they failed to alter the long-term downward trajectory of productivity growth. There is some research that suggests the boom experienced during the pandemic itself resulted from a one-time shift to remote working,[5] and indeed by 2024 the slowdown appeared to have resumed. And while the huge fiscal loosening of 2025 in the US, and to a lesser degree in Germany as well, was a boon to stock markets, which began the year with strong rallies, it was far from obvious that what would result from this new investment was a new surge in economic growth. Given the declining multiplier effect of government spending[6] and the fact that the US was now getting only 50 cents of added output from each new dollar of government spending, it was no surprise that economies defied the market optimism and continued slowing in the course of the year.

While the modern tale told by economic theory is that a few centuries ago, we entered a new age of endless innovation and economic growth, some recent scholarship has argued that the last two centuries may have been the exception rather than the rule.[7] In his magisterial book *The Rise and Fall of American Growth*, Robert Gordon argues that a small number of innovations, like the steam and internal combustion engines and electricity, truly transformed human productivity.[8] But rather than seeing technological innovation as a process that continually raises productivity, he contends that while it's possible that a few innovations radically transformed human output, we may never experience such transformations again. In other words, it's possible that our best days, technologically, are now behind us.

Consider the Internet. While celebrated in the 1990s as an epochal invention that would spread democracy and liberalism worldwide, bring people together and reduce conflict, and make economies super-efficient, even amid that hype, doubters pointed out that it represented less a new technology than an improvement on an existing – and very old – one: the telegraph. When it was invented, the telegraph truly eliminated distance and, for instance, allowed the emergence of nationwide and eventually global financial markets, genuinely transforming the economy. Ever since, some argue, every communications advance from the telephone to radio to television to the Internet merely built upon earlier advances. Meanwhile, the hype about the Internet and social media helping to create a more democratic, liberal and peaceful world has certainly come in for reconsideration.

Moreover, what may set today's technological developments apart from the early great breakthroughs may be that while the steam engine or electricity transformed the output of the entire economy, making almost everyone more productive, today's gains are possibly less diffused, with the benefits largely captured by a small class of intellectual-property owners – which helps explain the growing concentration of income and wealth among the very richest in Western countries.[9] Take Amazon, for instance. The very fact that researchers can claim that it has destroyed more jobs in retail than it creates would show it has raised labour productivity in this sector.[10] Nevertheless, its beneficial impact on the wider economy is contested, as there's evidence it also reduced competition and therefore has concentrated revenues in the company's hands, rather than raising the economy's productivity.[11] And while on balance the economy has continued to create jobs – after all, Amazon's employees create demand for services in the economy, from baristas to drivers – what may result is something that is called the Baumol-Bowen Cost Disease.[12] When a technology raises productivity within one sector of the economy, it generates demand for services in sectors that are less productive. The end result is that the technology does little to raise the overall labour productivity of the economy.

Admittedly, the fact that we haven't yet witnessed any evidence of a productivity transformation isn't proof that AI won't ultimately launch the next industrial revolution. If AI does transform the economy, it will be years before we know it, since, as we saw with earlier productivity transformations such as electrification, it took many years before the effects appeared in the economy. Equally, as we saw with the illusory tech boom of the late 1990s, any increase in productivity that does turn up in the meantime may prove fleeting and even have other causes. So, we can't say too much about this one yet.

All the same, however, we have been hearing this since at least Solow's 1980s dictum, and there comes a point where it becomes reasonable to ask those who insist a new industrial revolution is imminent if they are basing their claim on faith rather than facts. The people with the greatest confidence in new technology saving the day tend to be people who have great faith in new technology generally – and very often, they happen to be the people selling the product as well. Yet with each passing year that growth fails to take off, we have to begin contemplating other possibilities – including that the slowdown isn't the anomaly we need to explain, but the new norm we should expect.

One could go further and make a case that uncritical faith in the modern tale may actually help drive the Icarus effect. Belief that endless and rapid growth is the normal state of affairs, and that the long slowdown we've been experiencing is a temporary aberration, allows both politicians and their supporters to run up debts on the grounds that the return of growth will pay them down. But the downside risk, which receives insufficient attention, is that if the growth doesn't materialize, the resulting debt will act as a dead weight on the economy, mortgaging the future.

Beyond this, our discussion so far raises an even more radical possibility about the neoclassical utopia. A so-called shallower existence, characterized by material abundance and large-scale eradication of all forms of adversity, from even minor disease to falling asset prices, may actually make a society less dynamic and resilient, and therefore more vulnerable to shocks coming from nature. Or put differently, attempting to escape nature may well leave us at its mercy.

That, in short, would be the Icarus economy: the very ascent away from nature is what brings us back to earth. What insights might the natural sciences – in particular, those that most directly study human well-being, like medicine and psychology – offer us about this extraordinary idea?

The organic society

That a people's character and behaviour would change in fundamental ways that alter the economy's operation as they grow wealthier sits uneasily with conventional economic theory. The discipline prefers to see humans as 'representative agents' who, despite their diversity in talent, endowments and culture, nonetheless have the same basic drives and respond similarly to the same incentives, across time and space. The atomism of this approach can accept that humans will coalesce into a huge assortment of different institutional constellations, from fascism through to democracy – even if it does tend to believe some institutions, in particular liberal legal regimes that protect contracts and property rights, are evidently superior to others in generating utility. But the idea the atoms should themselves differ in essential ways is less easy to swallow.

However, the idea that individuals must be looked at through a different lens is more familiar in the natural sciences, and particularly in medicine, which after all sees humans as just one among countless living organisms, subject to many of the same laws and limitations as any other creature. One of the more intriguing developments of the last few years is the discovery of how prosperity has given rise to new medical conditions – in particular, allergies and autoimmune disorders. There's been a clear increase in both and cross-national research has found that their incidence rises with a society's income.[13] Anecdotally, this is something almost any person in a Western society who is past middle age can recall – that when they were children, they knew few people with allergies or food intolerances, but the number of people around them today who must regulate their diets or environment in order to avoid serious reactions has grown noticeably.

Initially, it was assumed this increase was simply due to the improved diagnostic techniques that accompanied economic development, or perhaps to increased exposure to pollutants due to industrialization. Some of this is clearly true, as many people had conditions that simply went unrecognized. But deeper research, including across societies, revealed these explanations to be inadequate. The fall of the Berlin Wall and opening up of Eastern Europe created a golden opportunity for researchers to study the impacts of air pollution on allergies, since the former Soviet bloc countries had lower-quality air.[14] To their surprise, though, they found that the incidence of allergies was higher in Western than Eastern Europe. Then, controlling diagnostic differentials across societies, another finding cemented the enigma: even allowing for the better diagnostic capabilities of developed societies, these conditions were simply not showing up with a similar degree of incidence in the developing world. To some degree, allergies and autoimmune disorders appeared to be a 'First World problem'.

Researchers looking into this enigma thus turned their attention to the 'hygiene hypothesis', the idea that hygiene practices in developed societies have removed many germs from daily circulation. The idea first arose in the late nineteenth century, when it was noticed that aristocrats and city dwellers were more susceptible to hay fever than farmers. The 'old friends' theory is that mammals co-evolved with organisms that served a vital task in priming the body's immunoregulation, and that their removal from the natural environment – or more to the point, the removal of humans from nature – interrupted this process, leaving humans more vulnerable.[15]

Initially used to explain the prevalence of allergies in Western societies, the hygiene hypothesis was subsequently tested as an explanation for the rising incidence of autoimmune disorders in rich countries,[16] and is now gaining widespread application.[17] The theory's upshot is that while cleaner, more controlled environments have reduced the incidence of some diseases, such sterility may have had an unintended consequence. Rather as a muscle needs activity to retain its mass, the immune system is kept primed by the experience of warding off new pathogens. When such pathogens become scarce, rather than atrophy as an unused muscle would, the immune system looks for new invaders that are otherwise innocuous – like allergens. Research has further shown that pre-natal and early childhood exposure to micro-organisms and parasites we would normally choose to avoid, like worms, may actually increase resistance to autoimmunity.[18]

This sheds interesting light on the Icarus effect. In the modern tale, embodied in conventional economic theory, the triumph of humanity has come from liberating itself from and then transcending nature altogether. What these findings in medical literature suggest is that the complete separation from nature makes humans more vulnerable to it. It may be that what is needed is not so much endless progress but some balance; liberation from nature's tyranny, but not complete separation from it.

Curiously, research on mental health reveals some equally interesting findings that would seem to square with this. It's well established that income rises that lift people out of poverty show a clear positive relationship with good mental health. Put differently, the poor-but-happy trope is a romantic delusion held by people who haven't experienced poverty. Equally, the impact of income loss on mental health is clearly negative: people who lose their job or suffer a decline in their income typically suffer mental health impacts. All of this offers clear support to the neoclassical premise that humans are utility maximizers, and that increasing their utility and decreasing their disutility produce clear improvements in contentment.

However, beyond a certain threshold, the linear relationship begins to break down. There is some evidence that beyond the point where one enjoys a high degree of income security and thus freedom from financial stress, further income gains show diminishing returns and may even lead to bad mental health outcomes.[19] It's also relatively established that at this point, what matters more to mental health outcomes is not further rises in absolute income, but its distribution. Which is to say that if some people's incomes are rising faster than others, mental health deteriorates, apparently due to two causes – one being the status anxiety of those who feel themselves excluded from the gains of economic growth, the second being the erosion of social capital as haves and relative have-nots mingle less, eroding interpersonal trust.[20]

This finding could help explain the paradox that has bewildered economists of late. Surveys of human contentment generally find a positive correlation between income and happiness, and every year the World Happiness Report puts out its ranking of the world's countries, with those reporting the highest level of happiness being among the richest countries, and those reporting the lowest being poor countries. Yet in their behaviour and political expression, the citizens of Western countries are showing rising discontent and anger, and are voting for politicians whose message is largely about how bad things have got. Economists struggle to account for this discrepancy and are left to speculate that perhaps people are being misinformed, or brainwashed by media, because the evidence seems incontrovertible. As the highly regarded former Federal Reserve governor Claudia Sahm said in a detailed comb through the evidence, 'most Americans are telling us they are not better off, but the data on people's finances are saying they are'.[21]

Aside from the possible methodological flaws in how we measure happiness – such as subjective surveys that are thus difficult to quantify[22] and may also bias findings in favour of rich countries, where the culture of individual contentment is more established[23] – it could be there's something going on here that we haven't picked up. Perhaps there's a threshold beyond which not only do further income gains produce diminishing returns, but they actually create vulnerabilities. There is some evidence of this, although it is admittedly murky: in a 2023 study, Daniel Kahneman found that human happiness plateaued at an income of around $75,000,[24] though in subsequent research he qualified this by saying the effect seemed to apply only to people who were already inclined to unhappiness. Research on happiness, which remains in its relative infancy, is finding myriad other factors that are associated with it. For instance, one puzzling finding that shows up repeatedly in surveys in developed countries is that conservative people are on average happier than their liberal counterparts, though nobody has yet worked out why.[25] Perhaps the most we can make of all this is that we may not yet have a good explanation as to what effect income has on happiness beyond the lower stages. We can say with confidence that poor people experience an improvement in their well-being as their income rises; but once they become rich, the results become more confusing, and it's possible that further riches may complicate their happiness or mental health, not unlike what happens with their physical health.

Another relevant thing to note is that interventions to improve mental health vary from developed to developing countries, with the latter relying more on community interventions to supplement the lack of state resources – a method that may produce outcomes which, if inferior in absolute terms, are relatively inexpensive.[26] Put differently, good mental health may become increasingly expensive to maintain as a society grows richer and, similar to what we found with the approach to pandemic prevention, the net outcome may be that lower-income countries have more resilient societies.

This kind of rich-isn't-necessarily-resilient framework has been applied to the study of societies as well, with some research finding that just as humans build resilience by experiencing adversity, so too may societies. One recent paper found that 'frequent disturbances enhance a population's capacity to resist and recover from later downturns', something that may well explain the differential performance of rich and poor societies during the pandemic.[27] Building upon this finding, we could further say that whereas a very poor individual will be vulnerable to illness, due to malnutrition and ill health, a very rich one might be so due to lack of fitness or sufficient priming against infection. The ideal situation may be to be prosperous enough to eat well and be healthy, but not so prosperous as to be sedentary and insulated from adversity.

This idea that both individuals and societies can rise to a point where they begin to fall backwards is one that the utility-maximizing model of neoclassical economic theory really can't accommodate. But there does exist a school of thought that attributes the loss of economic dynamism in Western societies to a sort of excess hygiene – namely, the sterilization of recessions, which has interrupted the natural life cycle that had once driven the ascent of capitalism. This would seem to suggest that endless and uninterrupted ascent goes against our nature, and that what is needed is the sort of renewal that comes in cycles of death and rebirth.

Brahma and Shiva in the economics lab

To see how this might work, it might help to go back to the beginning of our story. In the modern tale, those who had managed to distance themselves most from nature, the rich, had emancipated themselves from its tyranny whereas those closest to it, the poor of the developing world, would be thwarted by it. This was the moral narrative embraced by neoclassical economics from its nineteenth-century inception, and it envisioned a world of endless progress, measured in rising incomes and wealth. The fact that this isn't happening just now, and that if anything we may be going in reverse, evokes calls from economists for urgent measures to jump-start the economy.

But that may be the wrong diagnosis. There are other schools of economic thought, marginalized during the ascendancy of the neoclassical school (which eclipsed Keynesian economics after the 1960s to become dominant in university programmes) but that may now deserve reconsideration since they provide a different perspective on what's happening. In its early years in the late eighteenth and early nineteenth centuries, the discipline of economics, which started out as a branch of moral philosophy and later took the name 'political economy' – the term 'economics' being coined only much later – soon split into two dominant currents: British and German. These were loose constellations of thought, since the British school included French and Swiss thinkers while the German school proved popular in the young American republic that was formed after 1776.

Yet in their intellectual foundations, the differing British and German traditions would provide the contours of each school, as each bore the imprint of their respective philosophical ancestry. In keeping with the dominant currents of British philosophy at that time, the British school was rationalist, utilitarian, empiricist, and saw individuals as the sovereign constituents of societies. Societies, therefore, were conceived as social contracts – agreements among citizens to be bound by common rules and rulers in return for certain rights and privileges, including above all a right to security and, in keeping with British legal traditions, the right to the fruits of their labour, namely property. Pioneered by the Scottish philosopher Adam Smith, the British school was at root atomistic, seeing the economy as being an aggregation of more or less autonomous and free individuals who pulled together into larger groupings primarily because of the efficiency gains they could make in the process.

Over time, this atomism led the British school to gravitate to the science of theoretical physics, whose mathematical calculations to predict the behaviour of physical bodies was adapted to explain the economic behaviour of individual humans, and to identify ways of augmenting their material well-being. This focus on the individual thus gave rise to what would be called microeconomics, which saw the individual's decisions as the basis of an entire study.

The German school, which came to be known as Historicism or Institutionalism, arose in the early nineteenth century from a very different genealogy. Shaped by the then-strong influence of German Romanticism, the German school saw societies as living entities in their own right, and believed that they, rather than individuals, were what drove history. In contrast to the British focus on free trade liberating entrepreneurs to specialize in what they were best at, allowing the nation's economy to prosper as if guided by an invisible hand, the German school believed national economies had to be nurtured and integrated to be able to compete on a world stage dominated by first-movers. Hence, in contrast to the microeconomics of the English school, it leaned towards macroeconomics. This view of society in turn made the Historicists gravitate towards the science of biology rather than physics. Conceiving societies organically thus made them comfortable with the idea of natural cycles of rise and decline, ebb and flow, birth and rebirth.

A seminal influence in the development of this cyclical view of history was the philosopher Georg W.F. Hegel. Hegel conceived progress not as incremental steps towards new and higher equilibria, as would become the neoclassical view, but as a struggle in the realm of ideas between what has been translated as theses and antitheses. Starting in antiquity, when tyrants ruled, Hegel said the tyrant's complete freedom embodied a contradiction – namely, that it rested on the unfreedom of others – and that history advanced as the idea unfolded more widely: Greek tyranny giving way to Roman aristocracy, which, because it still denied the freedom of serfs and slaves, gave way through struggle to the equality of souls in Christianity, and so forth. This would then be adapted by the political economist Karl Marx, who would emerge as the principal rival to the emergent neoclassical school of economics in the second half of the nineteenth century and who substituted what he called historical materialism for Hegel's idealism.

Marx rejected the idea of progress embodied in what he called the bourgeois economics of the British school, which imagined humanity progressing in small steps, and instead saw history as driven by conflict, and specifically conflict between the classes, with the emergence of one mode of production requiring the destruction of its predecessor. Parting with Hegel, Marx posited that social classes rather than ideas moved history forward, thus opening the first chapter of *The Communist Manifesto* with the declaration 'The history of all hitherto existing society is the history of class struggles.' Driving the conflict were inherent contradictions between dominant and subordinate classes, which could only be resolved when the latter overthrew the former, moving history into the next mode of production. Ultimately, history would end with the defeat of capitalism by the working classes: Marx argued that the natural organization of a proletarian economy would be a classless one – and that without classes, the struggle driving history would come to an end.

This idea of an endpoint to the story of human ascent set the German school apart from the British one, since neoclassical economics would eventually come to see progress as endless (parting with earlier British theorists like John Stuart Mill who assumed it would reach a plateau). But while some German thinkers would see the cycle of rise and decline as terminal – Oswald Spengler's theory that the West was headed to the same decay that all great civilizations suffered would go on to have enormous influence – others saw it as being more of a continuous cycle, rather like the change of seasons that kept coming back around. As Friedrich Nietzsche put it in *The Genealogy of Morals*, the creation of a new temple demands the destruction of the old one.

There is some speculation that the idea was lifted from classical Indian philosophy, with its concept of creator and destroyer gods. The German Romantics had developed quite a keen interest in Sanskrit scholarship, and scholars like Johann Gottfried Herder and Heinrich Heine, who influenced them strongly, were themselves influenced by these ancient Eastern ideas. However, the notion of death giving rise to birth, and of the old needing to be killed by the new, is found in many different mythological traditions: the phoenix that rises from the ashes in classical Greek and Egyptian folklore, the idea of dying to be reborn in Christian teachings, the view of cycles that accord with the rhythms of nature, such as seasons of war and peace, death and life in the Psalms. At its heart it is a concept that is rooted in a naturalistic view of life, rather than the mechanistic one of neoclassical theory.

The idea as developed by Marx would later be built upon by Joseph Schumpeter who, however, gave it a novel twist. In his 1942 book *Capitalism, Socialism and Democracy*, Schumpeter elaborated on the Marxist theory of the business cycle. He agreed that crises were a motive force in history, and not necessarily something to be feared: when businesses failed, they released resources – capital, workers, market share – to more dynamic businesses, allowing them to grow faster. Schumpeter called this process creative destruction. Presenting an essentially evolutionary approach to economics, he saw the death of the old as a prerequisite to the birth of the new. As painful as bankruptcies and recessions were, they were necessary to the renewal of capitalism.

Befitting its Romantic ancestry, the Austrian school also departed from the neoclassical tradition in having an essentially heroic view of history, with the hero of the drama being the entrepreneur. Whereas neoclassical theory depicted a market in which supply, demand and prices would find their equilibrium naturally like atoms coalescing, Schumpeter portrayed a system in which everything depended on the great individual – the creative genius with the courage to risk failure in the pursuit of innovation and greatness. Not unlike Nietzsche's idea of the superman (*Übermensch*), Schumpeter and his colleagues believed that some people would rise to greatness and deserved to enjoy its fruit, while most humans would be happy to remain under-labourers, paid for their services. That's why when faced with the Great Depression, a time when most economists followed John Maynard Keynes in seeking to repair the economy and end human suffering, his Austrian rival Friedrich Hayek insisted that state intervention would interrupt the economy's natural process of repairing the damage done to the economy in the run-up to the 1929 Crash. To such a thinker, as to a Romantic, suffering was not a disutility to be eliminated; it was an inherent part of the creative process, whose elimination would end human intellectual, cultural and artistic advancement.

Creative destruction and the organic society

Mainstream economic theory allows for creative destruction. In *Why Nations Fail*, Daron Acemoglu and James Robinson argue that the slowdown of previously dynamic economies results from the ruling elites exploiting their power to frustrate the process of renewal, thereby entrenching their dominance.[28] They thus consider it a perverse outcome that points to a malfunctioning economy – like a lay-by on the highway of progress which, if exited, will enable humans to resume their endless ascent.

But in keeping with earlier adherents to cyclical theories of history, like Hegel and Marx, Schumpeter didn't consider the end of creative destruction to be an aberration, but rather the logical termination of the process. History for him had an endpoint. Despite being the demiurge that drove progress, he expected creative destruction to exhaust itself eventually. As the winners – the businesses and tycoons – of the evolutionary struggle grew more dominant, firms would become more bureaucratic and preoccupied with preserving their position. In this environment the entrepreneur would find himself isolated and constrained – what Nietzsche might have described as the victory of the last man over the superman.

This book raises the possibility that the economic slowdown and move into reversal that we are now seeing in some of the world's richest economies isn't an aberration, but a logical conclusion of the economic growth that creative destruction helped produce. Although the fact we no longer experience the kind of painful economic depressions our ancestors did is seen as a triumph of modern economics, it may be that we interrupted what is a natural process of renewal essential to a dynamic economy, in rather the same way that reducing infection, adversity and minor ailments may have weakened our resistance, or eliminating threats made us more vulnerable to them. We may, in short, have built an economy that runs contrary to our nature. For all our determination to transcend nature, it may still be getting the last laugh.

But while that might seem like a weakness on our part, it may yet be our biggest strength, and the key to solving our current crisis.

8

THE MIDDLE COURSE

In a 1963 speech, the British Labour Party leader and soon-to-be prime minister Harold Wilson declared that to accelerate the country's economic and social development, his government would harness the 'white heat' of a scientific revolution. 'Ninety-seven per cent of all the scientists who have ever lived in the history of the world since the days of Euclid, Pythagoras and Archimedes, are alive and at work today,' he told his party conference. 'You get some idea of the rate of progress we have to face.' It was a most eloquent rephrasing of the modern faith that had animated the last two centuries of dramatic economic growth: once again, we could look forward to scientific progress supercharging human material flourishing and taking it ever higher.

Which, in many ways, it did. Incomes rose, new cures for diseases were found, lifespans were further lengthened, more people went to university than ever before. And yet, at the very time Wilson was making his comments, Britain's economic growth rate was nearing its historic peak. It was shortly to begin a slow and steady decline towards the point we have reached today, when economic growth in Britain, as in most developed countries, is near zero. And as we've seen, the current trajectory suggests the only way forward, at least for now, is further downwards. The revolution Wilson foresaw never came – if by revolution we mean an age of dramatically rising economic output. In fact, the analogy used by Wilson to describe what he saw as the revolution's essence dovetails nicely with the one used throughout this book to help explain why: the white heat of Britain's prosperity may have already been starting to melt the wings that had carried the economy so high. Progress continued, but it would steadily slow to the point that some things started going backwards. Real incomes are now flat or falling, life expectancy may have peaked, public services are deteriorating even though taxes are rising.

Sixty years on, perhaps we should take stock of where we now stand. Britain, along with all Western countries, confronts two imminent threats to its future prosperity and well-being: a climate crisis and a growth crisis. Politicians, particularly those on the right, often present this as a choice. They tell us we can solve one or the other but not both, and that since solving the climate crisis will slow growth, we can't afford to do it. But what this book shows is that there probably is no such choice at all. If we opt not to stop the climate crisis, it will likely stop us. Call that a choice if you want, but I doubt few would take it – and even if they did, if they still insisted on ignoring the climate crisis, reality would bite even harder. As we've seen, this has already started to happen. Although the impact of extreme weather events on economic output and asset prices has so far been relatively limited in the rich countries, on the current trajectory things look set only to get worse.

We therefore face a toxic blend of steadily decelerating economic growth and negative shocks that look likely to repeatedly hinder or even set it back further. Those who still believe that human ingenuity alone will break out of this seeming doom loop continue to insist that we are on the cusp of the next technological revolution that, when it happens, will lift our economies so high we'll blow past all these problems, generating all the wealth and welfare we need to cope with climate change. But they've been saying that for nearly half a century now, and yet growth continues to slow.

Despite this, there are still grounds for optimism. This chapter will show how tackling the climate crisis may conceivably solve the growth crisis too. That may seem self-evident – any transition to a sustainable economic system that allows us to grow without further damaging the natural environment would get us past the external feedback loops to growth – but it's more than just arresting the negative shocks to growth that makes an energy revolution our best option: such a transition might also accelerate the development of emergent industries whose growth exceeds those of the old industries dependent on carbon-intensive energy, and which currently dominate developed economies.

That the two crises would find a common solution needn't surprise us either, since they both share a common cause – the ecological feedback loops of economic growth, which manifest themselves in both the external and internal environments. As we've seen, external loops produce exogenous shocks that inhibit further economic growth; internal ones give rise to behavioural changes that over time reduce economic dynamism as well as individual and social resilience, while imposing new costs on both the preservation of wealth and the protection of human well-being. In consequence, as an economy grows richer, its growth rate slows while its resilience to external shocks, along with its flexibility and adaptability, all decline. With growth rates consequently approaching zero in many Western countries, and with some having already crossed the threshold into degrowth, the increase in climate shocks will start tipping a rising number of them over the edge into long-term decline.

Thus, we now live in a world where the bulk of the wealth lies in the rich but stagnant and increasingly vulnerable West and most of the dynamism and resilience lies in the fast-growing but poor Global South. Suppose, then, we married them to one another? What if there were a wave of investment in the developing world that enabled it to leapfrog through the carbon-intensive growth of the last two centuries and straight into an age of renewable energy? This would prevent the developing world's future growth from pushing the planet past the point of no return for humanity's thriving, as is the current fear. Yet, as we'll go on to see, it might also prompt not only a new industrial revolution in the developing world but an economic renewal in developed countries as well.

We have both the means and the desire to make it happen – the means in the availability of capital, the desire in the huge and rapidly rising demand for renewable energy. The appetite for it in developing countries is immense. Countries that are still building their energy infrastructure would be happy to leapfrog the carbon age altogether and plunge into the energy transition for one simple reason: it is in countless ways the most cost-effective choice for them, one that promises potentially huge returns. While facilitated by governments, this transition is being driven mostly by ordinary people.

The developing world thus stands on the cusp of an energy revolution and buying into it would put the global economy on to a long-term path of sustainability, create new markets for Western goods and services, and add fuel to a nascent industrial revolution in the emergent new-economy sector of Western countries. China is already exploiting these opportunities. Thus, any Western countries choosing to avoid this transition will lock themselves out of these opportunities while doubling down on industrial technology that, in becoming relatively outdated and expensive, will make their exports less competitive in the future. The choice is therefore clear: choose decline or choose renewal.

Luckily, those countries that opt for the latter will find many eager and willing partners across the Global South.

A revolution from below

'It'll be a long time before electric vehicles come to Africa,' my colleague said one evening on a rooftop bar in Gaborone, the cosy, tidy capital of Botswana. I could see his point. Sitting in a rooftop bar – really, *the* rooftop bar, thirty storeys atop a small town that comprises mostly neat little homes fronting sleepy lanes – I scanned a horizon that stretched to a very distant point, the sun setting over the pastel-hued plain. In this vast land with many more cows than people, the distances in Botswana, as in much of Africa, make it seemingly inconceivable that a technology that requires regular charging points in remote areas could take hold here anytime soon.

However, just a few months later I was sitting in a conference room in Johannesburg, a sprawling, noisy, chaotic city in another land with improbably great distances and empty spaces, listening to a presentation of a radical new business about to sweep South Africa. In that short interim between my visit to Botswana and the seminar, the Chinese car manufacturer BYD had produced a low-cost hybrid car with a range of over 1,000 kilometres and a battery that could charge in five minutes. Electric vehicle (EV) technology was advancing at a breathtaking pace, with Western car executives returning to China after a couple of years of lockdowns astonished by the progress that had happened while they were away.

Having begun his career as a grid engineer with a side business interest in petrol stations, Joubert Roux, the CEO of the fledgling company, had spotted a potentially huge gap in the market. Like those of many developing countries, South Africa's electrical grid was collapsing under the weight of corruption and maladministration. While the government had re-secured control of the situation, restoring the state-owned electricity company was proving to be hugely expensive. Although most South Africans have access to electricity, the supply is unreliable and the bills costly. Especially in townships, connections can be cut for months due to unpaid bills in the community. Businesses often suffer interruptions during working hours, adding to production costs and lowering productivity. However, the country enjoys vast reserves of cheap, idle energy in sunlight, and Chinese EV technology had reached the point that it was now a viable option – provided those huge open spaces could be dotted with enough charging stations for long journeys.

Here's where Roux and his team of engineers came in. They envisioned a series of charging stations along the country's road network powered entirely by on-site solar micro-grids, equipped with diesel backup generators for the brief periods when sunlight was insufficient, located in such a way that no car would ever be more than 150 kilometres from a charge point. Having built a proof of concept in the north, Roux had now managed to attract the investment required to roll out the whole set across the rest of the country. 'The old model of grid-level electricity networks fuelled by large power stations is obsolete,' he told me. 'The future will be micro-grids, using local energy resources.' Rapid improvements in solar and battery technology had laid the groundwork for such a bottom-up revolution.

Across the developing world, where large utilities often fail and power cuts are widespread, middle-class households and businesses were installing solar panels on roofs in order to guarantee security of supply and reduce the gas bills required for noisy diesel generators. South Africa marched in the vanguard of this transition. In 2023, a year of long, rolling electricity blackouts had spurred the spontaneous installation of 4GW of rooftop solar generation – enough to put an end to the blackouts. The same thing happened in Pakistan that year, and for the same reasons – a failing public utility.[1] In 2023, Pakistan tripled its imports of solar panels and is now adding nearly 20GW per year to its electricity-generating capacity this way.

The rest of Africa is following suit, the continent having increased its imports of solar panels by 60 per cent over the last year.[2] This is producing huge increases in the electricity of many countries – 61 per cent over one year in Sierra Leone, 49 per cent in Chad, and over 5 per cent in some sixteen countries. Even if this revolution is being led at the micro-level, governments are keen to facilitate it, since for the most part these countries previously imported the fuel used to supply the old plants that generate their electricity, and they can thereby reduce their import bill. Vitally, that frightening scenario that briefly unfolded back at the time of the global financial crisis, when a lack of fuel risked causing a power grid to collapse in Jamaica, as in other countries, would hereby become a thing of the past.

Countries would now have their own, local, endless supply of energy inputs. Businesses like Roux's are popping up to meet the demand.

I'd already seen this kind of modular model build infrastructure across the developing world many years earlier. Way back in 1990, when I was a graduate student doing field research in Côte d'Ivoire, I'd come across what was then a similarly wild business proposal. In a country where telephones were a luxury and most people had to trek a mile or so to a public phone box in order to talk to anyone, I came across a young entrepreneur seeking an investor for his plan to build a mobile phone network. The idea at first struck me as preposterous: mobile phones were then a status indicator used mainly by the uber-rich or stockbrokers in Western countries, and the thought that they could spread through shanty towns in the Global South seemed beyond fanciful. But as that Ivoirien entrepreneur pointed out then, telephone networks in Western countries were largely monopolies that had saturated the market and had no reason to provide a competing product to their existing investment, whereas developing countries could leapfrog past the installation of extensive phone networks to install cellular towers and reach a new market. Very rapidly, subscription-based services, based on modest monthly fees, enabled mobile phones to become ubiquitous across the developing world. Mobiles came first to the periphery, and only then became widespread (and often more expensive still) in developed countries.

As happened with mobile technology, this distributed, micro-grid revolution is being led by the developing world. For example, Solar Panda is a firm created by Andy Keith, a Canadian entrepreneur who during a previous stint as a volunteer teacher in Africa had seen the dynamism in a continent widely viewed as backward. The firm has installed several hundred thousand nano-grids on rooftops across Kenya, many in remote villages where people's existing connection to the mobile-phone-based (and Kenyan-created) electronic payments system M-PESA enables the company to collect small monthly payments. So while the world has been transfixed by China's extraordinary transformation into becoming what many call the world's first electro-state – in 2023, China commissioned as much solar PV as the rest of the world[3] – many other developing countries have joined the rush. Brazil has installed so much new renewable capacity that it has almost completely decarbonized its energy grid.[4] EV sales in India have risen thirtyfold in just the last four years – even from a low base, a pace of increase that will decarbonize the transport system in a matter of years.[5] Ethiopia recently banned the importation of petrol-fuelled cars, determined to switch the country's fleet to local renewable energy. Driven by such rapid transformations, in the first half of 2025 the pace of global solar installation rose 64 per cent, continuing a multi-year trend in which the annual rate of expansion surpassed the previous years.[6]

It's easy enough to miss this when sitting in a Western country, listening to politicians say we can't afford the switch to renewable energy. But those countries that refuse to join the bandwagon won't prevent its rolling out; they will just find themselves stuck with dated, dirty, expensive energy technology that, like landline telephones, nobody else will want any more. When I asked Joubert Roux if the return of Donald Trump to the White House and his all-out assault on the energy transition had impeded his business in any way, he replied that the prospective investors he'd been courting in Europe stepped back, feeling the chill from DC, but that he then merely pivoted to Asia, securing the required investment. Andy Keith, the founder of Solar Panda, went further, saying Trump was inadvertently accelerating the energy transition with his anti-renewable Luddism. By removing a major buyer from the market – US investment in renewable energy declined by 36 per cent after he took office[7] – Trump has helped further lower prices on hardware, enabling more rapid and profitable adoption in developing countries.

Hitching a slow cart to a fast horse

Across the developing world, governments are doing their bit to facilitate this bottom-up revolution and Joubert Roux tells me he is getting a warm reception from governments elsewhere on the continent eager to see his micro-grid technology spread in their own countries. However, for the global energy transition to happen in time to prevent the downturn of the Western economies, it will need more – much more – capital than is currently available in most of these countries. McKinsey estimates that for the world economy to become net zero by 2050, it will need to invest some $275 trillion in physical assets, or roughly $9 trillion a year.[8] Currently the world spends nearly $6 trillion a year on physical assets, so the added funding would amount to about $3.5 trillion per year, or roughly $100 trillion over the next thirty years. In addition, of the nearly $6 trillion that is currently being spent each year on physical assets, nearly half is allocated to high-emissions assets, like power plants fuelled by fossil fuels, so that would need to be reallocated towards renewable energies.

While this may sound like a huge amount of money, it is in fact well within our means. Humanity has so far accumulated a pool of nearly $700 trillion in savings, of which some $450 trillion is liquid; which is to say, it can be relatively easily converted to cash and deployed to other ends.⁹ Every year, the world adds another $100 trillion to this output. Thus, a reallocation of a mere 1 per cent of assets would suffice to engineer this revolution, to say nothing of what could be allocated out of each year's output. (Bear in mind that those assets generally grow at an annual rate well above 1 per cent, so one wouldn't even need to dip into existing assets but merely reprioritize the distribution of future returns.)

Within the countries of the Global South, that process has already begun organically. In many countries households and businesses with the means to do so have already begun installing rooftop solar or creating micro-grids, as we've just seen. Within Africa, there are some $4 trillion of investable assets, roughly half a trillion of which are managed by pension funds. Nick Silver, a London-based actuary who has advised pension funds around the world, notes that managers in developing countries are typically committed to the principle of using national savings to spur development. Singapore's successful experiment with mobilizing domestic savings to stimulate rapid growth under Lee Kuan Yew, its first prime minister, serves as an inspiration in this regard; thus some, like South Africa's public pension fund, have already begun to invest in the energy transition.[10] Silver adds that managers of national funds also have the best local knowledge of the corporate and political landscape, and so their choices can then attract foreign investors into the space. That, too, seems to be happening. For instance, the founder of Solar Panda had no trouble attracting investors for his rollout of nano-grids.[11] Tom Rand, a venture capital fund manager who specializes in green energy industry, says that the pace of technological progress has been so rapid in the last few years that renewable energy will now beat fossil fuels at its own game, drawing investors in without further nudging.[12]

Nevertheless, accessing the immense funds of the developed world would supercharge this transition. There are over $60 trillion in the pension funds of the OECD countries alone, all of which are governed by national regulators.[13] By and large, these regulators prioritize a fiduciary requirement in their regulations – namely, obligating fund managers to obtain the highest possible returns for their beneficiaries. The logic behind this focus is obvious: ensuring sufficient asset growth to support the growing army of pensioners. In addition, pension funds in developed countries tend to be more risk-averse and have somewhat shorter horizons, given that so many of their members are now drawing a pension for which they must generate cash flow. But modest regulatory tweaks could prompt them to join this wave of investment in the energy transition.

Take the Canada Pension Plan (CPP), for instance, one of the world's biggest pension funds with over half a trillion dollars under management. Canada is the worst offender in the OECD when it comes to per capita carbon emissions and the CPP is doing its bit to maintain that lead, investing heavily in the country's fossil fuel industry and thereby perpetuating Canada's dependence on resource exports. With a slight tweak to its mandate to invest in the interests of all Canadians – similar to what its peer the Quebec pension fund has – the fund would end up shifting away from a dying industry to a future one.[14]

Admittedly, though, this transition will not be costless. There's a reason the CPP likes fossil fuel companies: they pay high dividends – in no small part because they invest less of their proceeds, given that future global demand for oil and gas looks set to diminish. While the long-term benefits of investments in green energy seem evident, their short-term yields can be lower. So, a fund under pressure to deliver high returns today may find it unable to meet its current level of commitments. In plain English, today's pensioners may experience some reduction in their incomes if we are to provide a future for today's workers and schoolchildren.

This brings us to game theory. In the dominant model of voting behaviour used today by most political consultants in Western democracies, nobody votes against their economic interest. Someone who will likely be dead before the worst effects of climate change hit will likely feel this adjustment as a net loss. And given that the rich countries are democracies, and moreover that pensioners are among the most reliable participants in elections, democratic leaders may be reluctant to exchange long-term gain for short-term pain. Which means the much needed reorientation of investment may not happen.

However, it's not clear whether this will be the decision-making calculus that governs people's behaviour. First, as this book has shown, the economic impacts of climate change don't lie in a distant future but are starting to manifest now, and will affect all but the oldest pensioners in their lifetimes. In recent years there has been growing talk of fund managers being stuck with 'stranded assets', which one report from the bank HSBC defined as assets 'that lose value or turn into liabilities before the end of their expected economic life',[15] like fossil fuels that remain in the ground because nobody wants them any more. There are already signs investors are starting to factor these future changes into their current pricing. Compare, for instance, two broad stock market indices: one of companies in the oil and gas sector, the other of companies in the renewable energy sector. The Dow Jones Oil and Gas Index peaked in the summer of 2014, and thereafter has essentially gone nowhere.[16] Over the same period, in contrast, the NASDAQ Clean Edge Green Energy Index has nearly doubled, and continues upwards.[17] Investors have already begun betting on the transition and even Donald Trump's concerted efforts to block renewable energy and 'drill baby drill' after he resumed office in 2025 failed to reverse these trends. Investors can see where the future lies.

To stranded and devalued assets, one can add the large set of assets whose values will be diminished by the sort of green swan events discussed in Chapter 6. Despite the rising incidence of extreme weather events that are destroying capital and knocking the resale values of real estate, we've yet to see a major repricing in asset markets. But that doesn't mean it isn't coming. Ben Keys, one of the leading experts on the financial risks of climate change, suggests we are already seeing the coalmine canary in insurance and reinsurance rates, which have risen in the US some 25 per cent in real terms since 2018. And while we've yet to see major moves in the real estate investment trust markets that track house prices, he warns that it is because such falls are obscured by countervailing cyclical trends. For instance, rising storm risks have sharply lowered house prices in parts of Florida, but the Covid real estate boom and baby boomers retiring to warmer climes have helped to soften overall price declines. Critically, however, Keys warns that what will set green swan events apart from earlier black swans is that when they do start to come, they will not be cyclical but structural. Unlike earlier crashes, which were caused by cyclical bubbles that, once they burst, eliminated excesses in the economy and put markets back on a sustainable path, for as long as climate change keeps worsening, the damage will persist and only deepen. It will be the scenario of an endless domestic war raised in Chapter 6.

In short, fund managers not only have to consider more than the existential risks of climate change, like social or even civilizational collapse, they also need to factor in the more mundane loss of value of their assets. Their future beneficiaries will suffer if they devote themselves solely to augmenting short-term returns, and they will likely do so sooner than previously expected. But beyond this purely financial reason that fund managers may want to reorient towards the energy transition more rapidly, it's not obvious that their existing beneficiaries would necessarily object to their prioritizing sustainable investment.

That's because everyday experience reveals people very often do, in fact, vote 'against their own interests'. The number of people who forwent substantial chunks of their income to put their children through education (everything from school and college fees to extra tuition, music lessons and sports club fees), or to help them get on the housing ladder or buy their first car is endless. But then, nobody suggested to them that they take a cut to their living standards. They were asked simply to make an investment in their children's future, something most people more than willingly do. Of course, the difference is that as they did with their education fees or helping their children get on the housing ladder, people freely and happily chose to invest in *their* children's future, not everyone else's.

But climate change is a collective-action problem that requires a collective-action solution – you just have to look at the billionaires trying desperately to get to Mars or building bunkers in New Zealand to realize nobody will escape its future harm. Arguably, what is needed is good leadership, from politicians who, when told that we can't afford the energy transition, show people they're not being asked to take a hit to their living standards, they're being asked to give their children a future. Much as the marketing of college funds and inheritance planning does.

Renewables and economic renewal

Besides, the opportunities that lie in this transition could potentially provide a new lease of life to Western economies. While most people working in the renewable energy industry say that China has largely captured the hardware segment – at least when it comes to solar panels, batteries and to some degree the EV sector as well – there remain many other areas where the field remains wide open. In addition to the fact that most jobs in the solar energy sector come after panels have been assembled, in the deployment of infrastructure,[18] Western countries enjoy a considerable comparative advantage in finance that will be essential to connecting such vast pools of capital to investment opportunities. While micro-grids and nano-grids require outlays of at most millions of dollars, and sometimes much less, Western pension funds and other such institutional investors are in the business of writing cheques in the hundreds of millions of dollars. A layer of intermediaries will thus be needed to connect big investors with the high-return yet small-scale projects that will bring about a rapid energy transition. Specifically, what will be required is the expertise to homogenize and bundle projects so that they can come under the roof of large investments, which are themselves ideally made tradeable on markets,[19] thereby creating a liquid pool of investments attractive to fund managers.

What fund managers in developing countries very often lack is the sort of technical expertise and experience in crafting such sophisticated investment products and then finding the clients for them. This is where Western financial houses have decades of experience in creating what are called collateralized securities of various types. For instance, packaging a huge number of small investments into baskets of homogenized products (in order to market them to investors used to making investments in the millions and even hundreds of millions of dollars, like Western pension funds) could create opportunities for venture capital firms, which are dominated by developed economies like the US. Venture capitalist Tom Rand says 'this is where the best young minds in the business' will be applying their talents in the coming years.

With the net zero sector growing much faster than the rest of the economy in several developed countries, the advantage of governments steering policy in favour of this emergent sector, at a time when demand in the fastest-growing part of the world economy is rising quickly – the developing world – seems evident. Even in oil- and gas-loving Canada, the green sector is expanding rapidly.[20] While most of it is so far focused on domestic industries, the opportunities in the developing world are multiplying fast. China is already aggressively entering this space, for instance by increasingly orienting EV exports[21] to these markets and using its Belt and Road Initiative to develop demand in South East Asia[22] for the outputs of its industries. Western countries can join this train, or they can watch it leave the station without them.

For those who still maintain, in the face of all evidence, that the energy transition will slow the economies of the West, the contrast between two countries with divergent approaches is revealing. In Canada, despite some efforts by the federal government to promote decarbonization, per capita emissions have continued rising, the fossil fuels industry holds sway and politicians nonetheless insist things are proceeding too fast. And yet, as we've seen, Canada is one of the rich countries already going backwards, as measured by per capita incomes. In contrast, Spain's government has aggressively promoted the transition,[23] and so from 2021 to 2024 the country expanded its renewable energy supply by 20 per cent, enjoying a 20 per cent reduction in energy costs as a result. This cost advantage has enabled the economy to grow strongly – more than the OECD average, and still running close to 3 per cent, better than even the US attained prior to its downturn but with nothing like the same run-up in debt (Spain's[24] fiscal deficit being half that of the US's[25]). Very importantly, this dynamism produced a more resilient economy. In recent years, both countries suffered from major ecological shocks – Canada's wildfires in 2023, Spain's catastrophic floods in 2024. Yet Spain bounced back more quickly,[26] and was growing above 3 per cent by year's end, whereas Canada continued to slide downwards.

We can't afford to stop climate change? The evidence suggests we can't afford *not* to.

CONCLUSION

This book has argued that economic growth alters nature: both the nature around us and the nature within us. This transformation then creates headwinds to further growth while raising its marginal costs, progressively reducing both the growth rate of the economy and societal resilience to adversity. As a result, faced with the exogenous shocks caused by the ecological effects of economic growth, like disease outbreaks or extreme weather, rich societies eventually begin to eat into their stock of wealth to preserve themselves, and thus grow poorer. Several countries have now begun to cross this threshold into degrowth.

Because the first signs of national degrowth are so recent that we must still regard the Icarus effect as a hypothesis, it is nonetheless one that appears at least as plausible as rival hypotheses which suggest that technology will lift economic growth rates back up. As that stagnation continues with each passing year or more countries tip over the edge into degrowth, the Icarus thesis will gain support. So, the conclusion would seem to be that, yes, if we continue on our course, the climate crisis will put a stop to what we're doing.

Except that – and this is the game-changer – developing countries are now growing rapidly and thus increasing their carbon emissions. By the time they reach the peak of their flight path and begin their own downturns, the planet will all but certainly have gone past a tipping point. Thus, left to its own devices, growth alone won't solve the climate crisis.

This book argues that it doesn't have to be this way – that there may be a way forward that both tackles the crisis and restores growth. By reallocating more of their accumulated capital towards accelerating the energy transition in developing countries, thereby minimizing the setbacks climate change is causing and will otherwise continue to cause, Western countries may be able to break out of this 'wealth trap' and thereby prevent further decline.

Treating the growth and climate crises as complementary rather than competing priorities may also be the only way to build an economic model that will not undermine itself. Admittedly, the challenge caused by the end of the Western world's dynamism is real enough on its own. Since 2007, on the eve of the global financial crisis, real per capita income in the EU has grown less than 1 per cent.[1] In Britain the rate has been less than half that;² in Canada it's barely above 0 per cent.³ Such a rapid slowing of economic growth has shown up in the rate of social progress as well. Life expectancy in the OECD, which had nearly doubled in developed countries over the previous century, peaked in 2014 at around eighty; since then it has more or less stagnated.⁴ All the same, merely raising growth rates won't itself solve the crisis of this moment.

To understand why not, consider a conversation that might have occurred had you been able to teleport yourself back to the nineteenth century to describe your life to one of your ancestors. You would tell them that in the twenty-first century, we had eradicated most childhood diseases and all but the most acute forms of pain; you would explain that we enjoyed a rich and abundant diet comprised of fresh food from around the world, a world we could now cross in a matter of hours; we'd see our children go to school until they are old enough to get well-paying jobs; and we'd all live twice as long as people in that century did – half the doubling thanks to dramatic reductions in child mortality, and half thanks to the fact everyone who made it out of childhood lived an average of twenty years longer.⁵ As if this didn't already sound to your ancestor like utopia, you'd then add that, unlike them, who would probably have little if any say in how they were governed, most of humanity was now given the opportunity to choose their leaders in competitive elections, during which politicians debated how we would spend the extra money our economy generated each year.

But then, things would take a bizarre turn. Your ancestor might respond that they would give anything to join that happy conversation, only for us to tell them it wasn't actually happy – that instead of a discussion packed with good news and fresh possibilities, we were instead angry, blaming each other for our sorry lot, and casting recriminations amid talk of revenge and violence. Meanwhile, many of us were turning against democracy, calling for strongmen to clean out the rot. In 2024, the V-Dem project, probably now the world's leading authority on the state of democracy, reported that the number of autocracies in the world had surpassed the number of democracies, turning the clock back decades.[6]

How on earth might we explain this paradox of prosperity to our ancestors: that despite all the sacrifices they might have made to ensure we had all these possibilities, despite being richer than they could have ever imagined possible, we are showing ourselves to be more miserable and resentful, at least in our politics? The clue can be found in the character of our continued talk of progress. Such talk suggests that things will get better, that artificial intelligence will enable us to create superhuman beings, that we're building rockets that will enable humans to vacation in space and colonize Mars, while millions are being invested in research to find how we might extend human life forever.[7] In contrast, in the talk outside these wealthy circles, as captured in the ubiquitous public opinion polls and vox-pop focus groups that pollsters and journalists conduct, what the rest of us are increasingly talking about is how unaffordable eggs have become, how the streets are dirty or poorly lit, how the trains are later and less reliable than they used to be, how getting a doctor's appointment is becoming a bigger challenge. As some talk about the inexorable march of progress, for others, things are going backwards.

Anyone can see that we have the resources to tackle the problems our society faces, not least the climate crisis. But the planet now produces more than enough food to feed all humanity, yet many still go hungry. Our problem is therefore no longer insufficiency, but inequity. Despite that glaringly obvious fact, when faced with the public's insistent demands for lower prices and better services, governments have kept falling back on the old playbook. 'I have three priorities for our economy,' said the ill-fated British prime minister Liz Truss at her 2022 party conference speech, 'growth, growth and growth.'[8] Not to be outdone, the Labour leader Keir Starmer told his party's 2023 conference that his government would restore Britain's economic growth,[9] a declaration later reiterated by his Chancellor Rachel Reeves when she said, 'Economic growth is the number one mission of this government.'[10] Donald Trump announced during the 2024 US election campaign that his plan would 'reignite explosive economic growth'.[11] This remains the standard playbook for Western leaders: to say they'll return growth to the rates of old in order to address public demands for fairness.

Their failure to do so, and the resulting public anger at the lack of results, has given rise to a street politics that searches for scapegoats, with immigrants, refugees and asylum seekers being the prime targets almost everywhere. But they aren't the problem.[12] Instead, those at the top of the income distribution hierarchy are still claiming the fruits of growth rates as if they were still rapid. However, since rapid growth hasn't materialized, the wealthy are doing it by taking more of the share of those at the bottom. Over recent decades, policies to inflate asset prices have made life costlier for those trying, for instance, to buy homes, and ever more government spending must be allocated to support them. Tax policies have favoured the rich, with one study of the US finding that billionaires paid an average of 24 per cent of their income in tax compared to the average of 30 per cent for the population as a whole.[13] One effect of this has been that wealth inequality has got worse across the developed world.

For example, in the US, in 1990, the top 1 per cent of the population owned 23 per cent of the wealth while the top 10 per cent owned 60 per cent.[14] Today, those figures are up to 31 per cent and 67 per cent respectively. Meanwhile, half the population today own a mere 2.5 per cent of its wealth. Research in Britain has found a similar pattern, with one study finding that, after falling dramatically over the course of the twentieth century, wealth inequality resumed widening from the 1990s.[15] Moreover, some of the gains have flown to non-working asset owners, which is to say pensioners: the wealth of older American households has risen much faster than the young.[16] In Britain, the incomes of pensioners have risen faster than those of working-age adults, and in France, pensioners even earn more than working people.[17]

Degrowth has in effect begun, because even in those Western countries whose per capita incomes haven't yet started declining, including the US, some citizens' quality of life is now being compromised for their better-off compatriots. Measures including policies that ensure the continued high growth rate of asset values amid slowing economies transfer wealth from workers to owners, enabling the living standards of the latter to keep rising at the rates of old. Many of these owners include well-off pensioners, whose funds can continue delivering them benefits as if growth remained high.

For example, the Canada Pension Plan forecasts real annual return on its investment of 3.7 per cent between now and the end of the century;[18] Australia's largest pension fund AustralianSuper projects 3.8 per cent over the next ten years;[19] Japan in 2024 raised its target from 1.7 per cent to 1.9 per cent;[20] and California State Teachers targets a nominal return each year of 7 per cent,[21] all growth rates that exceed those of the respective national economies by some margin. Meanwhile, in many countries taxes are rising to support the increase in state pensions: in the UK, for instance, the share of GDP devoted to the national pension[22] has risen from 3.5 per cent in 2000 to 5.1 per cent,[23] during which time the tax burden[24] compensated by rising from 32.7 per cent of GDP to 35.3 per cent. Reflecting this ability to capture a greater share of what income growth still exists, the rich have grown richer relative to the rest of the population in most OECD countries.[25]

But squeezing a growing slice from a pie that is scarcely expanding is not only a recipe for increasingly bitter politics – witness the rise of angry populists across the West – it doesn't tackle the root problem. It won't stop the pie from eventually getting smaller. At root, therefore, both the climate crisis and the political crises of Western societies stem not from lack of growth, but from inequity: the relative have-nots, both the citizens of the Global South who are successfully engineering their own rapid development and the victims of degrowth in the West who are demanding more from their governments and societies, are claiming back their share, tipping the old growth model into crisis. To build a sustainable economic system, we must tackle this inequity so as to put the world back on a growth path that will not undermine itself.

To that end, this book has proposed a wave of investment in the global energy transition, while noting that it will hit some in the short term – in particular, holders of pension assets. In effect, degrowth would then be shifted away from the more vulnerable and on to the shoulders of those most able to bear it. Unlike the existing degrowth, however, which risks sucking Western economies into downward spirals, this kind of managed degrowth would be a temporary measure that would ultimately produce a more sustainable economic model in which everyone rises together.

Funnily enough, this would compel economists to perhaps give degrowth thinkers a bit of credit, since they at least address the subject of equity and fairness. But the significant upshot is that to rise to the challenges of this new economy, to stretch their imaginations to find solutions to the problems we have created, economists will probably do well to go back to being ethicists and not merely the 'value neutral' scientists they have long imagined themselves to be. After all, moral philosophers is what they were in the beginning, in the days of Adam Smith, John Stuart Mill and Karl Marx. Those ethicists, in turn, were rooted in the morality of the ancient tales. Crafting an economic theory that allows for a world of endless but slower growth than in the past amounts to saying that humans need to strive for a world in which they fly towards the sun while accepting they may not reach it.

This book opened with a metaphor about nature having the last laugh at humans. The idea that what makes us human is an ability to transcend nature altogether has arguably only been the preserve of a relative handful of science-fiction enthusiasts and tech bros. The same claim can be made of the economy – that fundamentally, human genius has found ways to enhance the output of nature. Capitalism arose when humans found new ways of appropriating nature's capital and converting it into use value: opening a seam in the earth and extracting the minerals may have been a feat of engineering ingenuity, but claiming the full value as a human product, when humans were merely adding value, overstated our achievement. Arguably, many – perhaps even most – of the great achievements of the age of progress have resulted not from overcoming nature but rather from working *with* it so as to enhance its operations. This has been true of vaccination, the elimination of water-borne diseases with public sanitation, and improved nutrition, to mention just a few. We have to give nature more credit for our achievements. Because as we've seen, if we don't give nature its due, it may just claim it.

The plot of the modern tale we outlined in the first chapter – that the progress of the last few centuries came from, and contributed to, humans transcending nature and liberating themselves from its constraints – has been upended. The hero who managed to rise beyond nature found himself suddenly vulnerable to its revenge, whereas the protagonist still living at nature's mercy was spared the worst of its wrath. Like a kill switch in our make-up, which activates when we fly too high.

In its original telling, Daedalus, the father of Icarus, was the hero we were to look up to. The master artificer used his talent to transcend nature's limits but warned his son not to try to rise beyond it, for fear he would fall back to earth. That may be the lesson we take from Icarus economics: that we have extraordinary abilities to make nature work for us, but only for as long as we recognize we remain part of it and can never fully emancipate ourselves from it. And, being the social animals that we are, part of that nature is the recognition that we are all in this together – that if we build a model in which we can all rise together, the centre of both our politics and our economics will once again hold.

NOTES

Introduction

1. Peter Heather and I elaborate the concept of the West and how it evolved in our book *Why Empires Fall* (London: Allen Lane, 2023), but as a shorthand we can regard all the members of the OECD that are developed economies as the main constituents of the West.
2. https://ourworldindata.org/grapher/global-average-gdp-per-capita-over-the-long-run
3. https://ourworldindata.org/maternal-mortality
4. https://ourworldindata.org/child-mortality-in-the-past#:~:text=Infant%20mortality%20rates%20in%20the%20past&text=Across%20the%20entire%20historical%20sample,Around%20half%20died%20as%20children
5. https://www.ft.com/content/3f3fd905-92a4-4361-ba4d-11bf222b2c33
6. https://www.economist.com/finance-and-economics/2020/12/08/the-pandemic-could-give-way-to-an-era-of-rapid-productivity-growth
7. https://www.mckinsey.com/industries/public-sector/our-insights/will-productivity-and-growth-return-after-the-covid-19-crisis
8. John Rapley, 'Are we on the cusp of another roaring twenties?', *Globe and Mail*, 1 January 2021. https://www.theglobeandmail.com/opinion/article-are-we-on-the-cusp-of-another-roaring-twenties/
9. https://www.munichre.com/en/company/media-relations/media-information-and-corporate-news/media-information/2025/natural-disaster-figures-2024.html
10. https://www.nature.com/articles/s43247-023-01173-x

1 The Story of Our Ascent

1. The FAO estimates that global per capita food production now stands at around 3,000 calories per day. https://openknowledge.fao.org/server/api/core/bitstreams/15b3480c-65c3-486a-bbcd-5a75f3ddb056/content

ICARUS ECONOMICS   239

2. https://www.who.int/news/item/24-07-2024-hunger-numbers-stubbornly-high-for-three-consecutive-years-as-global-crises-deepen--un-report#:~:text=This%20projection%20closely%20resembles%20the,percent%20in%20high%2Dincome%20countries
3. https://ourworldindata.org/what-is-economic-growth
4. https://philarchive.org/archive/KAPTTO-4
5. New York: D. Appleton and Company, 1875, p.vi. https://www.google.ca/books/edition/History_of_the_Conflict_Between_Religion/e-3ffDpJ_woC?hl=en&gbpv=1&pg=PA2&printsec=frontcover
6. Charles Dickens and Richard Horne, 'The Great Exhibition and the Little One', *Household Words*, 1851. https://www.napoleon.org/en/history-of-the-two-empires/articles/the-great-exhibition-and-the-little-one-from-household-words/
7. See his interview with Aaron Bastani. https://www.youtube.com/watch?v=bjlqWHXrTak
8. https://timotheeparrique.com/a-response-to-the-financial-times-a-few-points-of-clarification-about-degrowth/
9. https://www.penguin.co.uk/books/429710/doughnut-economics-by-kate-raworth/9781847941398
10. https://brankomilanovic.substack.com/p/degrowth-solving-the-impasse-by-magical
11. See A.C. Pigou in *The Economic Journal* 12,47 (September 1902), pp.374–5.

2 Transcending Nature's Limits

1. http://news.bbc.co.uk/onthisday/hi/dates/stories/july/20/newsid_3728000/3728225.stm
2. *The Life and Times of the Thunderbolt Kid* (London: Doubleday, 2006), p.5.
3. W.W. Rostow's *The Stages of Economic Growth*, which would be the bible of 'modernization theory' and form the basis of American diplomacy towards the developing world in the Kennedy and Johnson administrations, was published at the tail end of this period, in 1960.
4. https://ourworldindata.org/co2-emissions
5. In his 1977 book *The Silent Revolution*, Ronald Inglehart contrasted the 'materialist' values of working-class parties, which remained preoccupied with material advancement, with the 'post-materialist' values of a new left that, amid seemingly endless abundance, was liberated from material want to pursue new ideals like sexual freedom or self-actualization.
6. https://pages.mtu.edu/~asmayer/rural_sustain/governance/Hardin%201968.pdf

7. *The Anti-Politics Machine: Development, Depoliticization, and Bureaucratic Power in Lesotho* (Cambridge: Cambridge University Press, 1990).
8. https://core.ac.uk/download/pdf/144880881.pdf
9. See https://www.epa.gov/greenvehicles/50-years-epas-automotive-trends-report#:~:text=The%20good%20news%20%2D%2D%20New,Chart%20graphic
10. Richard M. Adams, 'Global Climate Change and Agriculture: An Economic Perspective,' *American Journal of Agricultural Economics* 71,5 (1989), p.1273. https://www.jstor.org/stable/pdf/1243120.pdf?casa_token=z6K5duBf27UAAAAA:RKh67k1_ma-YIsPmptpK2jB2g6DvQu5J0-0uEgbPYecFSmKJrzYEWWJDlnH5TDeUHul9XCOtKsV8RdHdnR4BKRFFfNx3OXBN-cV7hT0XkVMQ
11. R.M. Adams, et al., 'Implications of Global Climate Change for Western Agriculture', *Western Journal of Agricultural Economics* 13,2 (1988), p.353. https://www.jstor.org/stable/40987996
12. *National Income, 1929–1932* (United States, 1934), p.7. This 'letter' was prepared by Kuznets on behalf of the Acting Secretary of Commerce. https://fraser.stlouisfed.org/title/national-income-1929-1932-971?page=2
13. Whereas President Jimmy Carter had once said 'shared sacrifice' would see America through a crisis, Clinton's neoliberal rhetoric parted with this old morality and said the pursuit of self-interest would solve all problems.
14. John Rapley, *Twilight of the Money Gods* (London: Simon & Schuster, 2017), p.312.
15. https://www.jstor.org/stable/2880417
16. William D. Nordhaus, 'Expert Opinion on Climate Change', *American Scientist* 82,1 (1994), p.48. https://www.jstor.org/stable/pdf/29775100.pdf?casa_token=GNQcaW-cw_0AAAAA:lz1tsrsp6TTgCP1Emd3-VB9Fu0oyPJzJLDlWhEVl46aAugvpF8BxbcKRylKCRUjVFf2kyLXEhrAAsIJPnTeivQ5haMX_ydlVCl77Q12MCJtKDI3LggKyOg
17. https://gain.nd.edu/our-work/country-index/rankings/
18. Yamoussoukro became the country's official capital in 1983, but most government offices and all the business head offices remain in Abidjan.
19. https://www.nature.com/articles/s43017-024-00624-z#Sec12
20. See Brent M. Simpson and Gaye Burpee, 'Agricultural Extension and Adaptation Under the "New Normal" of Climate Change', in Walter Leal Filho (ed.), *Handbook of Climate Change Adaptation* (Berlin: Springer, 2014).

3 The Pandemic Paradox

1. Even the theory that the virus entered human circulation after a leak from a Wuhan research laboratory, which remains a minority opinion among scientists, wouldn't alter its origin in the wilderness: the Gain-of-Function research said to be taking place in the lab consists of strengthening zoonotic viruses that risk entering human circulation in order to prepare treatments for them. The research exists precisely to head off the problem that has resulted from human encroachment into hitherto-isolated regions.
2. https://www.theguardian.com/world/2020/apr/02/global-battle-coronavirus-equipment-masks-tests
3. Chris Jackson and Jason Lu, Revisiting Covid Scarring in Emerging Markets, IMF Working Paper WP/23/162 (August 2023).
4. John Authers, 'How Risky is Covid? Here's a Way to Look at it', Bloomberg.com, 8 July 2020. https://www.bloomberg.com/opinion/articles/2020-07-08/covid-19-how-to-weigh-the-market-risks-kccu3uyp?embedded-checkout=true
5. See, for instance, https://www.mediaandminorities.org/assets/media-contributions/Bleich2020JSAfrica.pdf
6. The data in the above section is drawn from https://ourworldindata.org/coronavirus
7. https://wdi.worldbank.org/table/3.12
8. https://wid.world/document/developing-countries-in-times-of-covid-comparing-inequality-impacts-and-policy-responses-world-inequality-lab-issue-brief-2021-01/
9. https://apps.who.int/nha/database/PHC_Country_profile/Index/en
10. https://www.oecd.org/en/publications/2023/11health-at-a-glance-2023_e04f8239/full-report/health-expenditure-on-primary-healthcare_bf72cd24.html
11. https://www.umaza.edu.ar/archivos/files/Metaanalisis%20sobre%20agua,%20sanitizacion%20y%20medidas%20higi%C3%A9nicas.pdf
12. https://www.gov.uk/government/speeches/pm-economy-speech-30-june-2020
13. Kenichi Ohmae, 'Managing in a Borderless World', *Harvard Business Review*, May–June 1989. https://hbr.org/1989/05/managing-in-a-borderless-world
14. Georgia Collins, 'KPMG: Global Manufacturing Outlook Following COVID-19', 31 August 2021. https://manufacturingdigital.com/smart-manufacturing/kpmg-global-manufacturing-outlook-following-covid-19

15. Markus Keck and Patrick Sakdapolrak, 'What is Social Resilience? Lessons Learned and a Way Forward', *Erdkunde* 67,1 (2013), p.7.
16. Brigit Maguire and Patrick Hagan, 'Disasters and Communities: Understanding Social Resilience', *Australian Journal of Emergency Management* 22,2 (May 2007), pp.16–20.
17. Keck and Sakdapolrak, 2013, p.11.
18. New Brunswick: Transaction Books, 1988.
19. https://pmc.ncbi.nlm.nih.gov/articles/PMC7888611/
20. N.A. Marshall, 2010, in studying US and Australian ranchers, found that overestimating their ability to cope with effects of climate change actually made them more vulnerable to its effects. https://www.sciencedirect.com/science/article/abs/pii/S0959378009000880
21. Hyman P. Minsky, *Stabilizing an Unstable Economy* (New Haven: Yale University Press, 1966), p.237.

4 The Wealth Paradox

1. Which is to say, the developed market economies of the OECD. These mostly comprise West European countries and some former British 'settler' colonies – the US, Canada, Australia and New Zealand – while postwar Japan and South Korea are usually added to the mix for falling into the US-dominated postwar order.
2. This isn't standard practice in growth accounting, which is revealing since it arguably flatters the already-weak performance of the developed economies, given that the share of new debt in most developing countries is considerably lower.
3. https://fred.stlouisfed.org/series/NYGDPPCAPKDJPN
4. https://fred.stlouisfed.org/series/NYGDPPCAPKDFRA
5. https://fred.stlouisfed.org/series/NYGDPPCAPKDDEU
6. https://fred.stlouisfed.org/series/NYGDPPCAPKDGBR
7. https://fred.stlouisfed.org/series/NYGDPPCAPKDCAN
8. https://tradingeconomics.com/united-states/government-debt
9. https://x.com/KobeissiLetter/status/1814678667353862162
10. Ibid.
11. Ibid.
12. https://www.cbo.gov/system/files/2024-03/59711-Long-Term-Outlook-2024.pdf
13. https://www.ft.com/content/7071e5cb-b9ad-490e-8702-44e9434aab1f
14. https://unherd.com/newsroom/a-us-stock-market-crash-is-brewing/
15. All data in the above paragraph drawn from World Bank, World Development Indicators.

16. https://hdr.undp.org/system/files/documents/global-report-document/hdr2025reporten.pdf
17. https://adamtooze.substack.com/p/chartbook-404-violence-and-dedevelopment?utm_campaign=email-half-post&r=59u5y&utm_source=substack&utm_medium=email
18. Data from World Bank, World Development Indicators.
19. See IMF, World Economic Outlook update, July 2025. https://www.imf.org/en/Publications/WEO/Issues/2025/07/29/world-economic-outlook-update-july-2025
20. https://www.afdb.org/en/news-and-events/press-releases/africa-dominates-list-worlds-20-fastest-growing-economies-2024-african-development-bank-says-macroeconomic-report-68751
21. https://ourworldindata.org/grapher/median-age
22. https://www.nippon.com/en/japan-data/h00727/
23. Ibid.
24. https://www.academia.edu/66263208/When_Education_Expenditure_Matters_An_Empirical_Analysis_of_Recent_International_Data
25. https://www.oecd.org/en/topics/education-attainment.html#:~:text=Educational%20attainment%20of%2025%2D64,20%20percentage%20points%20favouring%20women
26. Ha Joon Chang has argued that this higher education has done little to raise productivity because most university graduates end up doing jobs for which a degree is unnecessary, with employers imposing degree requirements merely as a sorting mechanism – what he calls degree inflation.
27. https://ourworldindata.org/life-expectancy
28. https://uk.bookshop.org/p/books/the-rise-and-fall-of-american-growth-the-u-s-standard-of-living-since-the-civil-war-robert-j-gordon/3433250?ean=9780691175805
29. https://jonathanhaidt.com/anxious-generation/
30. https://www.mckinsey.com/mgi/our-research/the-power-of-one-how-standout-firms-grow-national-productivity
31. https://www.ft.com/content/4e5f3e36-cdab-4661-90e2-0c0d94a2100e
32. See World Bank data.
33. Data from World Bank, World Development Indicators.
34. https://www.youtube.com/watch?v=vZmgZGIZtiM
35. https://www.scmp.com/magazines/style/news-trends/article/3091222/japan-1980s-when-tokyos-imperial-palace-was-worth-more
36. https://www.macrotrends.net/global-metrics/countries/jpn/japan/gdp-gross-domestic-product
37. https://data.worldbank.org/indicator/GC.DOD.TOTL.GD.ZS?locations=JP

38. https://www.ceicdata.com/en/indicator/canada/private-debt--of-nominal-gdp
39. See *Why Empires Fall*.
40. https://www.oecd.org/en/data/indicators/general-government-financial-wealth.html
41. New York: PublicAffairs, 2020.
42. Bank for International Settlements, Macroprudential policies to mitigate housing market risks (CGFS Paper no. 69), December 2023. https://www.bis.org/publ/cgfs69.pdf
43. https://www.ft.com/content/fadfbd9e-29ca-4d53-b69a-2497cc3ed95d

5 The Wealth Trap

1. In particular, free universal education, especially for girls, can accelerate a society's demographic transition.
2. https://obr.uk/frs/fiscal-risks-and-sustainability-july-2025/
3. https://fred.stlouisfed.org/series/PSAVERT
4. https://www.sciencedirect.com/science/article/abs/pii/S0922142512000333
5. https://tradingeconomics.com/ethiopia/gross-savings-percent-of-gdp-wb-data.html
6. https://tradingeconomics.com/india/gross-savings-percent-of-gdp-wb-data.html
7. https://tradingeconomics.com/indonesia/gross-domestic-savings-percent-of-gdp-wb-data.html
8. https://tradingeconomics.com/china/gross-savings-percent-of-gdp-wb-data.html#:~:text=Gross%20savings%20(%25%20of%20GDP)%20in%20China%20was%20reported%20at,compiled%20from%20officially%20recognized%20sources
9. See https://www.oecd.org/content/dam/oecd/en/publications/reports/2025/06/understanding-the-weakness-in-business-investment_1e03ea2e/89bd437d-en.pdf
10. See, for example, https://d1wqtxts1xzle7.cloudfront.net/88025158/showpaperpdf-libre.pdf?1656363736=&response-content-disposition=inline%3B+filename%3DRisk_Taking_in_Financial_Decisions_as_a.pdf&Expires=1755787802&Signature=G-Rd~T7tGP0EhMzU52WonOMWbr~KEFG~eukobab2pWyEJwZuWZEPTDxiqRkm4QS61I64Oa7J~iya4YaROaGKfkGLc7f4i-fwSiiuatIaopPaom2b-SAr0TSdfA6RBGlHspPHGkGgqZ-CNc34S2HPkxlQ2UQ2z~5lU8bmWlRdsOyBcA1P7qa1ejU-yBbb6KgBKnKtM4MlY4FtJCVDPerfyzVZSgVBbQyYBc3pmQnqyxWFrXOB3bjyZvqWoVMgUNc

MvVkXb6Jdk0S9iKyJRS7XUhO1eAaTd7AnJqXf2h0HhMoxV6W 48KtCFlpqHrRPqMiGDxDEVDrKfclJjjnB9hUoI6w__&Key-Pair-Id=APKAJLOHF5GGSLRBV4ZA (See also https://www.academia.edu/82258600/Risk_Taking_in_Financial_Decisions_as_a_Function_of_Age_Gender_Mediating_Role_of_Loss_Aversion_and_Regret)

11. https://d1wqtxts1xzle7.cloudfront.net/104710661/7b57b50e58ca1452 03f4893e269facf91963-libre.pdf?1690995378=&response-content-disposition=inline%3B+filename%3DDemography_of_Risk_Aversion. pdf &Expires=1755787203&Signature=bh1fZlUNzJZ1tSqMbTXnD FN1r0qi~vMWkEpBBoLMQCxMBiauUH4ShK3MSKGd12aq1Uz qLP6aS9a9mm23~4tGbTpVOEUm32GCAQqGkwFXHU~Z pdgvGqHv31HPQDndMp1tGImQBmuLEvsPPto9WYTbzyx 1OdLP1VZLrAgW72wqIooDntRn8wCWj9Kqt9xc1fJ61xJtpw fkry1HsdgdxRS5ViL3gMyazy5Se~Efy7959wKBaCItt18yD4ke4 vJ4~y9UfgfaqgxhyopjSTz~ZKcbJTHnU25e1zTl0B7xXH-80z9OUQ_ iCT8Z1Wze2otCOCfRAuFWnARUvjj3HO8CGH6qHUg__&K ey-Pair-Id=APKAJLOHF5GGSLRBV4ZA

12. https://cdn.prod.website-files.com/62306a0b42f386df612fe 5b9/67ae1254b4f4ffe6e38a3b0f_Open%20for%20Business%20or%20 Up%20for%20Sale%20final%20draft.pdf

13. There's also growing evidence of an increase in the role of activist investors (https://www.ft.com/content/95008728-986c-4dcf-95aa-16fbb4ef4bfd), who tend to favour distribution over accumulation (https://corpgov.law.harvard.edu/2016/06/23/activist-investors-and-target-identification/#:~:text=On%20average%2C%20activist%20 investors%20accumulate,to%20generate%20substantial%20shareholder%20value), which they often do by running down capital (cost-cutting) or running up debt. Given that the risk of activist investing overlaps with the rise of the private equity industry, and that the private equity industry has in turn grown in importance largely because of the growth of pension funds (https://unherd.com/2023/10/is-private-equity-too-big-to-fail/), which are its biggest investors, it may be that the investment model that is gaining salience is one that runs down existing wealth rather than creating new wealth.

14. https://www.theguardian.com/commentisfree/2025/jul/07/europe-financial-sector-house-prices-politics

15. https://newsletter.economics.utoronto.ca/wp-content/uploads/Zaleski-2025-Give-People-and-They-Will-Have-Kids-Housing-and-Fertility-in-the-US.pdf

16. See https://academic.oup.com/restud/article-abstract/79/4/1559/1573 571?login=fals

17. See https://www.huduser.gov/periodicals/ushmc/summer94/summer94.

html#:~:text=Since%201960%20the%20homeownership%20rate,adjustment%20by%20the%20Census%20Bureau. And https://www.historyextra.com/period/modern/a-brief-history-of-home-ownership-in-britain/
18. https://www.cambridge.org/core/journals/american-political-science-review/article/abs/does-property-ownership-lead-to-participation-in-local-politics-evidence-from-property-records-and-meeting-minutes/E3BAEB8B52992D8FCF37FF3166BB2E77
19. https://conversationswithtyler.com/episodes/ezra-klein-3/
20. https://journals.sagepub.com/doi/full/10.1177/0010414019897418
21. https://fred.stlouisfed.org/series/MSPUS
22. https://onlinelibrary.wiley.com/doi/pdf/10.1111/1467-923X.13301
23. See Figure A1 in https://www.wipo.int/edocs/pubdocs/en/wipo-pub-941-2023-en-world-intellectual-property-indicators-2023.pdf
24. See Figure A6 in ibid.
25. See Figure A11 in ibid.
26. https://www.mckinsey.com/mgi/our-research/investing-in-productivity-growth?utm_source=substack&utm_medium=email
27. https://www.globalpropertyguide.com/most-expensive-cities
28. The World Bank's Ease of Doing Business Index, which charted such changes, was discontinued in 2021 after an audit raised questions about the quality of data. Nonetheless, the broad picture that the previous two decades of reports revealed was of many developing countries turning themselves into more attractive places to conduct business.
29. See https://www.oxfordeconomics.com/wp-content/uploads/2025/05/OEGCI2025.pdf
30. https://www.intellinews.com/emerging-market-tiger-cities-power-global-growth-prospects-403386/
31. Estimates of world income over time are compiled in the Angus Maddison tables, which are briefly summarized and put into graphical form in Our World in Data. https://ourworldindata.org/grapher/gdp-per-capita-maddison-project-database?time=1800
32. See *Why Empires Fall*.
33. https://fred.stlouisfed.org/series/CP
34. https://fred.stlouisfed.org/series/GDP
35. https://www.macrotrends.net/2324/sp-500-historical-chart-data
36. https://fred.stlouisfed.org/series/GDP
37. https://fred.stlouisfed.org/series/BOGZ1FL192090005Q
38. https://data-explorer.oecd.org/vis?df[ds]=DisseminateFinalDMZ&df[id]=DSD_NAMAIN1%40DF_QNA_EXPENDITURE_GROWTH_OECD&df[ag]=OECD.SDD.NAD&dq=Q..CAN%2BDEU%2BFRA%2BGBR%2BITA%2BJPN%2BUSA%2BO

ECD%2BG7%2BEA20.S1..B1GQ......G1%2BGY.&pd=2007-Q1%2C&to[TIME_PERIOD]=false&vw=tb
39. https://www.ons.gov.uk/economy/nationalaccounts/uksectoraccounts/bulletins/nationalbalancesheet/1995to2021#:~:text=UK%20net%20worth,-Net%20worth%20shows&text=products%2C%20and%20land.-,The%20UK's%20net%20worth%20increased%20by%20%C2%A31.0%20trillion%20to,of%20the%20UK's%20net%20worth
40. See https://www.bis.org/publ/cgfs66.htm
41. https://www.ft.com/content/e12a1eee-2571-4ae5-bc91-cc17ee7f40d0
42. https://seafordmacro.com/wp-content/uploads/2022/12/Seaford-Macro-Inflation-Brief-01-22.pdf
43. For further discussion see https://centaur.reading.ac.uk/89576/1/EPSR-2019-0090.R2_Proof_hi.pdf and https://scholar.google.co.za/scholar?hl=en&as_sdt=0%2C5&q=inglehart+norris+2016&btnG=
44. In 2025, Canada reduced its target for immigrants from 500,000 to just under 400,000. https://nationalpost.com/news/canada/canada-immigration-report

6 The Kill Switch Within

1. https://www.ft.com/content/f709d0d6-a540-471f-8c18-4e3366089152
2. https://ourworldindata.org/grapher/co-emissions-per-capita#:~:text=What%20you%20should%20know%20about,GCB
3. https://www.carbonbrief.org/analysis-which-countries-are-historically-responsible-for-climate-change/
4. https://pubmed.ncbi.nlm.nih.gov/12288594/
5. https://nymag.com/intelligencer/2021/11/climate-change-reparations.html
6. https://www.cbc.ca/news/science/how-canadians-can-cut-carbon-footprints-1.6202194
7. See https://www.jasonhickel.org/blog/2017/11/19/why-branko-milanovic-is-wrong-about-de-growth
8. https://www.un.org/en/climatechange/science/climate-issues/degrees-matter
9. https://iopscience.iop.org/article/10.1088/1748-9326/adbd58
10. See https://eprints.lse.ac.uk/117270/1/The_Missing_Risks_of_Climate_Change_author_manuscript.pdf
11. https://www.pnas.org/doi/full/10.1073/pnas.2103081118
12. See https://www.theactuary.com/2025/01/09/amber-alert-introducing-planetary-solvency; https://www.nature.com/articles/s41586-024-07219-0#:~:text=Specifically%2C%20macroeconomic%20impacts%20

have%20been,temperature2%2C3%2C18; https://www.nber.org/papers/w32450?utm_campaign=ntwh&utm_medium=email&utm_source=ntwg7 ; https://iopscience.iop.org/article/10.1088/1748-9326/adbd58

13. https://www.nber.org/papers/w32450?utm_campaign=ntwh&utm_medium=email&utm_source=ntwg7
14. https://www.nature.com/articles/s41586-024-07219-0
15. https://www.bnnbloomberg.ca/
16. https://www150.statcan.gc.ca/n1/daily-quotidien/250228/dq250228a-eng.htm
17. J. Childs, et al., 'Emerging Zoonoses', Special issue *Emerging Infectious Diseases* 4,3 (July–September 1998), p.454.
18. https://www.ft.com/content/599c87da-7920-4832-87de-98934cb5cbc4
19. *The Black Swan: The Impact of the Highly Improbable* (New York: Random House, 2007).
20. See https://www.theguardian.com/science/2020/mar/25/coronavirus-exposes-the-problems-and-pitfalls-of-modelling
21. https://www.ft.com/content/506f5a03-8520-40e1-aee3-a6e6427f68c0
22. One 2025 study estimates that such superbugs could reduce global economic output by nearly 1%, and that it would be rich countries that bear most of the cost. https://www.cgdev.org/sites/default/files/forecasting-fallout-amr-economic-impacts-antimicrobial-resistance-humans.pdf
23. See BIS/Banque de France paper, *The Green Swan: Central Banking and Financial Stability on the Age of Climate Change*, 2020.
24. See Simpson and Burpee, 2014; and see Munich Re report that estimates the rising cost globally of natural catastrophes resulting from climate change. https://www.munichre.com/en/company/media-relations/media-information-and-corporate-news/media-information/2025/natural-disaster-figures-2024.html
25. https://www.climate.gov/news-features/blogs/beyond-data/2023-historic-year-us-billion-dollar-weather-and-climate-disasters#:~:text=Adding%20the%202023%20events%20to,376%20events%20exceeds%20%242.660%20trillion
26. https://www.eea.europa.eu/en/analysis/indicators/economic-losses-from-climate-related#:~:text=The%20most%20expensive%20hazards%20during,(EUR%2017%20billion)%2C%20the
27. https://www.cbc.ca/news/canada/climate-change-insurance-fires-1.6863796
28. https://wid.world/www-site/uploads/2023/01/CBV2023-ClimateInequalityReport-1.pdf
29. https://library.wmo.int/doc_num.php?explnum_id=10989

30. See Exhibit 2 in https://www.aon.com/getmedia/f34ec133-3175-406c-9e0b-25cea768c5cf/20230125-weather-climate-catastrophe-insight.pdf#page=7
31. https://www.ft.com/content/c1d1ee7f-f34a-490d-bbd6-95b895ffd33e
32. https://www.ft.com/content/272fac7a-9d8f-4afe-a489-0ea6b5837ee5
33. Ibid.
34. Benjamin Keys, Wharton School, University of Pennsylvania, Interview, 3 July 2025.
35. https://www.ft.com/content/32b588a7-b470-4012-8bc2-f9eea3f17902
36. One study of the Los Angeles area estimated that up to 20% of electrical capacity could be lost in future heatwaves, which in the absence of mitigation strategies could cause widespread power failures. See https://www.sciencedirect.com/science/article/abs/pii/S0301421518308590?fr=RR-2&ref=pdf_download&rr=999274c5f951a88f
37. See https://pmc.ncbi.nlm.nih.gov/articles/PMC9882910/pdf/nihms-1866303.pdf
38. https://www.sciencedirect.com/science/article/pii/S0959378017304077
39. https://www.ft.com/content/9e5df375-650d-492e-ba51-fb5a34e6ddd6
40. https://www.axios.com/2024/03/25/climate-change-inflation
41. https://www.nature.com/articles/s41586-025-09085-w
42. https://www.nature.com/articles/s43247-023-01173-x#:~:text=Future%20warming%20to%20amplify%20pressures,have%20consequences%20for%20future%20inflation
43. https://www.nature.com/articles/s43247-023-01173-x#:~:text=Future%20warming%20to%20amplify%20pressures,have%20consequences%20for%20future%20inflation
44. https://fred.stlouisfed.org/series/FLSTHPI
45. Benjamin Keys, Wharton School, University of Pennsylvania, Interview, 3 July 2025.
46. See Exhibit 15 in https://www.aon.com/getmedia/f34ec133-3175-406c-9e0b-25cea768c5cf/20230125-weather-climate-catastrophe-insight.pdf#page=7
47. https://www.nature.com/articles/s41586-025-09085-w
48. The strongest losses are expected to come in moderate-temperature belts that, for instance, grow wheat, like the US and southern Africa.
49. Moreover, in contrast to the research on productivity, which generally converges on an ideal workplace temperature in the mid-20s, the research is far less conclusive about what an ideal night-time temperature would be; one of the most effective strategies for managing sleep environment appears to be altering bedding (https://www.mdpi.

com/2071-1050/13/16/9099), and improved airflow (https://onlinelibrary.wiley.com/doi/abs/10.1111/ina.12599) is usually found to be beneficial. See, for instance, http://ibse.hk/SBS5222/Building_and_Environment_v43y2008p70-81.pdf

50. https://pmc.ncbi.nlm.nih.gov/articles/PMC9882910/pdf/nihms-1866303.pdf
51. https://www.thesun.co.uk/news/33704792/net-zero-killing-uk-industry-farage/
52. See https://www.theguardian.com/environment/2025/feb/24/britain-net-zero-economy-booming-cbi-green-sector-jobs-energy-security#:~:text=The%20net%20zero%20businesses%20accounted,a%209%25%20jump%20in%202023

7 The Icarus Economy

1. See https://www.brookings.edu/wp-content/uploads/2020/01/WP57-Collis_Brynjolfsson_updated.pdf
2. https://timesmachine.nytimes.com/timesmachine/1987/07/12/issue.html. A recent paper by some Federal Reserve economists underscored Solow's view, arguing that the postwar productivity boom in Western countries was due to an exceptional demographic feature, and that there was no evidence computerization did anything to raise labour's hourly output. https://www.richmondfed.org/publications/research/economic_brief/2024/eb_24-25#:~:text=In%201987%2C%20economist%20Robert%20Solow,but%20in%20the%20productivity%20statistics.%22
3. The attempts by economists to factor addiction into decision-making models itself offers a rich literature. See, for example, https://www.sciencedirect.com/science/article/abs/pii/B9780080440569500440
4. https://www.cambridge.org/core/journals/experimental-economics/article/abs/economic-effects-of-facebook/6C5CF85813CAFB52AB15DDA131C171AF
5. https://www.nber.org/papers/w30267
6. This declining multiplier effect is not confined to Western economies, as China is also exhibiting a similar trend: its multiplier may remain positive, but it is declining and in some cases may be below one, suggesting that every yuan of government spending may produce less than that in added output.
7. https://press.princeton.edu/books/paperback/9780691175805/the-rise-and-fall-of-american-growth?srsltid=AfmBOore_4I7jFJ_Wv50mREVzD2vhcDaYisP_631kN4Rc_lvjw8Xh3DZ
8. Princeton: Princeton University Press, 2017.

9. https://www.cbpp.org/research/poverty-and-inequality/a-guide-to-statistics-on-historical-trends-in-income-inequality#:~:text=Wealth%20%E2%80%94%20the%20value%20of%20a,over%20the%20past%2035%20years
10. http://www.kavalacapital.com/content/20201201-Rapport_ecommerce.pdf
11. https://yalelawjournal.org/pdf/e.710.Khan.805_zuvfyyeh.pdf
12. https://pages.stern.nyu.edu/~wbaumol/OnThePerformingArtsTheAnatomyOfTheirEcoProbs.pdf
13. Fan Cao, et al., 'Global burden and cross-country inequalities in autoimmune diseases from 1990 to 2019', *Autoimmunity Reviews* 22,6, June 2023.
14. Perta I. Pfefferle, et al., 'The Hygiene Hypothesis: Learning from but not living in the past', *Frontiers in Immunology* Mini Review, 16 March 2021.
15. See Graham A.W. Rook, 'Hygiene Hypothesis and Autoimmune Diseases', *Clinical Reviews in Allergy and Immunology* 42 (2012), pp.5–15.
16. Jean-François Bach, 'Revisiting the Hygiene Hypothesis in the Context of Autoimmunity', *Frontiers in Immunology* 11 (2020).
17. Giuseppe Murdaca, et al., 'Hygiene hypothesis and autoimmune diseases: A narrative review of clinical evidences and mechanisms', *Autoimmunity Reviews* 20,7 (July 2021).
18. See Lenny Djuardi, et al., 'Immunological Footprint: The Development of a Child's Immune System in Environments Rich in Microorganisms and Parasites', *Parasitology* 138,12 (July 2011), pp.1508–18.
19. See this case study from China: Chao Li, 'More income, less depression? Revisiting the nonlinear and heterogeneous relationship between income and mental health', *Psychology* 13 (14 December 2022).
20. See Richard Layte, 'The Association Between Income Inequality and Mental Health: Testing Status Anxiety, Social Capital, and Neo-Materialist Explanations', *European Sociological Review* 28,4 (August 2012), pp.498–511.
21. See https://stayathomemacro.substack.com/p/most-americans-are-better-off-financially
22. See https://www.nber.org/system/files/working_papers/w19950/w19950.pdf
23. The idea is that people with a less individualistic identity might under-report their own happiness if they feel others around them are not so happy: see https://link.springer.com/article/10.1007/s10902-022-00588-1
24. https://www.pnas.org/doi/10.1073/pnas.2208661120
25. One recent paper suggests the intriguing possibility that it

results from under-reporting of unhappiness due to the stigma associated with mental health. https://journals.plos.org/plosone/article?id=10.1371%2Fjournal.pone.0321573&s=03
26. See, for instance, Kwame McKenzie, et al., 'Learning from low income countries: mental health', *BMJ* 329 (2004), pp.1138–40.
27. Philip Riris, et al., 'Frequent disturbances enhanced the resilience of past human populations', *Nature* 629 (2024), pp.837–42.
28. New York: Crown Publishers, 2012.

8 The Middle Course

1. https://ember-energy.org/latest-insights/the-first-evidence-of-a-take-off-in-solar-in-africa/
2. Ibid.
3. https://www.iea.org/reports/renewables-2023/executive-summary
4. https://ember-energy.org/latest-insights/brazil-rises-as-g20-renewables-powerhouse/#:~:text=89%25%20of%20Brazil's%20electricity%20came,were%20below%20the%20global%20average
5. https://www.iea.org/data-and-statistics/data-tools/global-ev-data-explorer
6. https://x.com/ryankatzrosene/status/1965063638202655226
7. https://www.axios.com/2025/08/26/us-investments-renewable-energy-projects-numbers?utm_source=newsletter&utm_medium=email&utm_campaign=newsletter_axiosam&stream=top
8. https://www.mckinsey.com/capabilities/sustainability/our-insights/the-net-zero-transition-what-it-would-cost-what-it-could-bring#/
9. https://www.forcegood.org/frontend/img/CF4Greport-2024/Capital%20as%20a%20Force%20for%20Good,%20Report,%202024.pdf
10. https://energycapitalpower.com/africa-eyes-pension-funds-to-drive-energy-infrastructure-investment/
11. Interview with Andy Keith, 25 August 2025.
12. Tom Rand, managing partner, ArcTern Ventures, 25 August 2025.
13. https://www.oecd.org/content/dam/oecd/en/topics/policy-sub-issues/asset-backed-pensions/PMF%202025%20-%20Preliminary%202024.pdf
14. When asked what he thought of the campaign by Canadian activists for a change in the CPP mandate, the actuary Nick Silver said he 'agreed with extreme prejudice'.
15. See https://www.pembina.org/blog/climate-change-financial-risk-stranded-assets
16. https://www.marketwatch.com/investing/index/dwcogs

17. https://www.marketwatch.com/investing/index/nsdqcels?countrycode=xx
18. https://www.sustainabilitybynumbers.com/p/clean-energy-imports-jobs?utm_source=post-email-title&publication_id=1199196&post_id=161721185&utm_campaign=email-post-title&isFreemail=true&r=59u5y&triedRedirect=true
19. Tom Rand, managing partner, ArcTern Ventures, 25 August 2025.
20. https://www.the-big-green-machine.com/
21. https://www.ft.com/content/743915a7-5994-48a3-80b2-13570570ccda?desktop=true&segmentId=7c8f09b9-9b61-4fbb-9430-9208a9e233c8#myft:notification:daily-email:content
22. https://www.iiss.org/online-analysis/online-analysis/2024/07/chinas-evolving-belt-and-road-initiative-in-southeast-asia/
23. https://www.bbvaresearch.com/en/publicaciones/spain-reaping-the-benefits-of-renewable-energy-in-the-spanish-economy/
24. https://www.oecd.org/content/dam/oecd/en/publications/reports/2025/06/government-at-a-glance-2025-country-notes_9de36e82/spain_3c7b5028/57f4ebd0-en.pdf
25. https://www.cbo.gov/topics/budget#:~:text=CBO%20estimates%20that%20if%20the,in%20August%20or%20September%202025.&text=The%20federal%20deficit%20in%202024,percent%20of%20gross%20domestic%20product
26. https://data.worldbank.org/indicator/NY.GDP.MKTP.KD.ZG?locations=ES-CA&name_desc=true

Conclusion

1. https://fred.stlouisfed.org/series/NYGDPPCAPKDEUU
2. https://fred.stlouisfed.org/series/NYGDPPCAPKDGBR
3. https://fred.stlouisfed.org/series/NYGDPPCAPKDCAN
4. https://data.worldbank.org/indicator/SP.DYN.LE00.IN?locations=OE-CA
5. See https://ourworldindata.org/its-not-just-about-child-mortality-life-expectancy-improved-at-all-ages
6. See https://www.v-dem.net/documents/60/V-dem-dr__2025_lowres.pdf
7. Bryan Johnson is probably the individual most closely associated with this project, though those who have looked at his extreme regimen for eternal life have sometimes been left wondering why one would want it.
8. https://just-access.org/transcript-of-truss-conservative-conference-speech/
9. https://labour.org.uk/updates/press-releases/keir-starmers-speech-at-labour-conference/

10. https://www.gov.uk/government/speeches/chancellor-vows-to-go-further-and-faster-to-kickstart-economic-growth
11. https://www.politico.com/news/2024/09/05/trump-economy-00177543
12. Indeed, in my previous book, with Peter Heather (*Why Empires Fall*), we argued they were the *solution*, or at least a big part of it.
13. https://papers.ssrn.com/sol3/papers.cfm?abstract_id=5404069
14. https://www.federalreserve.gov/releases/z1/dataviz/dfa/distribute/chart/#range:1989.4,2025.2;quarter:143;series:Net%20worth;demographic:networth;population:all;units:levels
15. https://www.resolutionfoundation.org/app/uploads/2020/12/The-UKs-wealth-distribution.pdf
16. https://www.nber.org/papers/w34131
17. https://www.ft.com/content/d419bd2d-a6ba-44a5-a93a-1276f3e5d2d7
18. https://www.cppinvestments.com/newsroom/cpp-investments-net-assets-total-714-4-billion-at-2025-fiscal-year-end/#:~:text=The%20Chief%20Actuary's%20projections%20are,of%20Canadian%20consumer%20price%20inflation
19. https://www.australiansuper.com/why-choose-us/mysuper-dashboard
20. https://www.asiaasset.com/post/29109-japanwelfareminsitry-gte-1203
21. https://www.calstrs.com/calstrs-earns-8-5-net-return-exceeds-benchmark-in-fiscal-year-2024-25#:~:text=The%202024%E2%80%9325%20return%20keeps,interest%20rates%20and%20geopolitical%20uncertainty
22. https://obr.uk/forecasts-in-depth/tax-by-tax-spend-by-spend/welfare-spending-pensioner-benefits/#:~:text=Pensioner%20benefit%20spending%20is%20forecast,5.1%20per%20cent%20of%20GDP
23. Ibid.
24. https://www.oecd.org/content/dam/oecd/en/topics/policy-sub-issues/global-tax-revenues/revenue-statistics-united-kingdom.pdf
25. https://pmc.ncbi.nlm.nih.gov/articles/PMC9340753/#Sec8

INDEX

Abidjan, Côte d'Ivoire, 63–5
Acemoglu, Daron, 112, 201
Africa, 100–101, 169
   Covid-19 and, 77, 78–81
   'lost decade', 109
   renewable energy, 212–17
ageing societies, 124–32, 134
agriculture
   climate change and, 58, 61, 167
   industrialization of, 67, 70, 146, 159–60
air conditioning, 165–6, 171
air pollution, 188
alien life, 49
allergies, 187–9
Alphabet Inc., 96
Amazon, 96, 183–4
antibiotic-resistant superbugs, 146, 161
Apple, 96
Argentina, 78, 138
Arrow, Kenneth, 127
artificial intelligence (AI), 96, 99, 177–8, 184
Australia, 78, 234
Austrian school of economics, 200
autoimmune disorders, 187–9

Babylonian mythology, 20
Bank for International Settlements, 161–2
Baumol-Bowen Cost Disease, 184
Belgium, 43
Benin, 100
Bernanke, Ben, 133
'Big Yellow Taxi' (song), 47
bird flu, 68
Black Death, 5, 74
'black swan' events, 159–61
Blake, William, 44
Bloomberg, 75
Bolivia, 78
Bosnia and Herzegovina, 79
Botswana, 209–10
Brazil, 214

British school of economics, 195–9
Brundtland Commission, 52, 54
Brynjolfsson, Erik, 177–8
Bryson, Bill, 42
Buffett, Warren, 120
Bulgaria, 79
BYD car manufacturer, 210

California State Teachers, 234
Cambodia, 100
Canaanite mythology, 20
Canada, 8, 66, 96, 115–16, 142, 150, 157, 170–71
   climate change and, 63, 163, 218–19, 225–6
   Covid-19 and, 72
   immigration, 145
   population, 144
Canada Pension Plan (CPP), 218–19, 234
capitalism, 120–22, 200, 236
Capitalism, Socialism and Democracy (Schumpeter), 200
carbon tax, 60–61
Carlyle, Thomas, 29
Central African Republic, 62, 100
Chad, 62, 100, 212
ChatGPT, 178
Cherokee people, 20
China, 18, 21, 24, 46, 66, 79, 101, 109–10, 138, 153, 209
   Belt and Road Initiative, 225
   Communist Party, 110
   Covid-19, 68, 81
   electric vehicles, 210–11
   renewable energy, 214, 223–5
   savings rates, 126
   technological innovation, 135
Christianity, 20, 199
Churchill, Winston, 127
cities, 136–9, 166
climate change, 9–11, 14–17, 33, 37–8, 49–51, 60–62, 66–7, 147–73
   carbon emissions, 149–53, 160, 168, 219
   climate whiplash, 66–7
   economics of, 15–17, 51, 56–63, 151–2, 154–8, 164–9
   extreme weather events, 10, 38, 50, 67, 161, 163–6, 168, 170–71, 221
   Global Adaptation Index, 62–3
   global warming, 49–50, 60–62, 66–7, 149–50, 155
   politics and, 172, 204–6
   real estate and, 165–6, 169
   rich/poor countries and, 146–58, 163–4, 169–70, 228
   see also renewable energy
climate economics, 62–3

Clinton, Bill, 60
colonies/ colonialism, 29–30, 43, 109, 110–11
  see also imperial eras
Columbus, Christopher, 4
communism, 41, 198
Communist Manifesto, The (Marx), 198
Confucianism, 21
Congo, 65
conservatism, 192
consumerism, 42–3, 45–6
Côte d'Ivoire, 63–5, 213
Covid-19 pandemic, 2, 5–9, 67, 68–82, 87–96, 105, 107, 145, 158–60, 162–3
  cost of, 79–80
  death rates, 78–80
  economic rebound, 6–9, 74–6, 93, 94–6, 99–10, 107–8
  rich/poor countries, 71–5, 77–82, 87, 91–2, 99–102
  vaccines, 74
'creative destruction' of economies, 120, 200–202

Daedalus, 237
Daly, Herman, 51
debt, 115–19
Deficit Myth: Modern Monetary Theory and the Birth of the People's Economy, The (Kelton), 117
deforestisation, 67, 146, 159
degrowth, 26–, 388, 52, 54, 141–2, 150, 207, 227, 233–5
democracy, 230
Deng Xiaoping, 110
Denmark, 78, 145
dependency ratio, 103, 126, 129
Development Dictionary: A Guide to Knowledge as Power, The (Sachs), 53
Dickens, Charles, 23–4
Diet for a Small Planet (Lappé), 46
Dow Jones Oil and Gas Index, 220
Draghi, Mario, 133
Drake equation, 49
Draper, John William, 22

Earth Day, 46
Ebola virus, 81
ecological economics, 51–2
ecological resilience, 90
economic bubbles, 120–21
economic efficiency, 88–90
economic growth, 15–17, 27–31, 38–9, 108–10, 141–2, 174–6, 185, 228–9
  climate change and, 15–17, 51, 56–62, 206–8, 216
  degrowth, 26–8, 52, 141–2, 150, 207, 227, 233–5
  economic revolution, 17–19, 25
  'golden age' (1948–73), 41–5, 108–9

growth/degrowth polarity, 15–17
  politics and, 144–5, 204–5, 230–32
  rich/poor countries, 109–14, 138, 180
  sclerotic growth, 175
  Solow-Swan model, 112, 142, 179, 184
Economist, The, 6
education spending, 104–5
Egyptian mythology, 199
electric vehicles, 209–11, 214–15
empires *see* imperial eras
Encountering Development: The Making and Unmaking of the Third World (Escobar), 53
endogenous growth school, 112–13
energy, 32–3, 66, 208–9
  consumption, 45
  fossil fuels, 55–6, 216, 218–20
  investment in renewables, 216–22
  net zero, 172, 216, 225
  prices, 55–6
  renewable energy, 208–26
Enlightenment, 22, 36
environmentalism, 46–7, 60
Escobar, Arturo, 53
Ethiopia, 100, 126, 214
  famine (1984), 66, 77
evolution, 22
extreme weather events, 10, 38, 50, 67, 161, 163–6, 168, 170–71, 221

Facebook, 180–81
Farage, Nigel, 172
Ferguson, James, 53
financial crashes, 92, 120–21, 131, 161, 167
  global financial crisis (2008), 108, 110, 121, 132–3, 143, 162, 212
  Wall Street Crash (1929), 131–2, 201
Financial Times, 6, 99
Florida, 169, 221
food production, cost of, 10, 161
fractional-reserve banking, 118
France, 43, 52, 95–6, 142
free market, 56–7
Friedman, Milton, 52, 133
Friends of the Earth, 46
fungal infections, 161

Gaia hypothesis, 3, 50–51, 66, 70, 147
GDP, 28, 53–4, 95–6, 107–8
Genealogy of Morals, The (Nietzsche), 199
Germany, 96, 142, 143, 176, 181
  German school of economics, 195–9
  national debt, 116–17

postwar Germany, 40–41
Romanticism, 196, 199
Gini coefficient, 59
Global Adaptation Index, 62–3
global financial crisis (2008) *see* financial crashes
global hunger, 18, 48
global pandemics, 158–62
Global South, 36, 62, 65–6, 73–5, 101, 208–13, 217, 234–5
GNP, 58–9
'golden age' (1948–73), 41–5, 47–8
Gordon, Robert, 182
Graduate, The (film), 45
Grapes of Wrath, The (Steinbeck), 130
Great Depression, 130, 201
Great Exhibition (1851), 23
Greek mythology, 20, 31, 199
green swan events, 161, 221–2
greenhouse effect, 49–50
Greenpeace, 46
Guyana, 101

happiness, 191–3
Hardin, Garrett, 47–8
Harold and Maude (film), 45
Hayek, Friedrich, 201
healthcare, 83–7
Heather, Peter, 110–11
Hegel, Georg W.F., 197–8, 202
Heine, Heinrich, 199
Herder, Johann Gottfried, 199

Hickel, Jason, 27, 150
Hindu mythology, 20
Historicism, 196–7
History of the Conflict between Religion and Science (Draper), 22
HIV, 67, 81
homeownership *see* real estate
Horne, Richard, 23–4
HSBC, 220
Hugo, Victor, 110
Hurricane Melissa (October 2025), 87
Huxley, T.H., 22
'hygiene hypothesis', 188–9

Icarus effect, 11–13, 147–8, 185–6, 189, 227–8
Icarus myth, 31, 124, 175, 237
immigration, 103, 144–5
imperial eras, 7, 17, 36, 43, 62, 103, 110–12, 138, 152
    rise and fall of empires, 110–12
import substituting (IS) policies, 109
income, 17, 28, 114, 138, 233
    global per capita, 4, 30
    happiness and, 190–93
India, 18, 66, 100, 110, 126, 137, 138, 153, 214
Indian philosophy, 199
Indonesia, 126, 153
Industrial Revolution, 16, 18, 22–6, 32, 35, 43–5, 59, 108

next industrial revolution,
    179–82
industrial society, 44–6
inequity, 230–31
infant mortality, 4–5
inflation, 140, 168
Institutionalism, 196–7
International Monetary Fund
    (IMF), 75
Internet, 177–9, 181, 182–3
Italy, 69, 78
    life expectancy, 125

Jakarta, 136–7
Jamaica, 82–4, 132–3, 212
Japan, 96, 103–4, 120
    economic stagnation, 114–15
    life expectancy, 125
    national debt, 116
    pension funds, 234
    savings rate, 126
    technological innovation,
        135
Johannesburg, South Africa,
    34–5, 210
Johnson, Boris, 69, 88
Judaism, 20
'just-in-time' inventory
    management, 89

Kahneman, Daniel, 192
Keith, Andy, 214, 215, 218
Kelton, Stephanie, 117
Kenya, 214
Keynes, John Maynard, 201
Keynesian economics, 30, 195

Keys, Benjamin (Ben), 165, 221
Klein, Ezra, 131
KPMG, 90
Kristofferson, Kris, 134
Kuznets, Simon, 58–9
Kuznets curve, 58–9

Labour Party, 145, 176
Latin America, 79
Lee Kuan Yew, 217
Lesotho Highlands Dam
    project, 53
Libya, 78
life expectancy, 84, 105–6,
    124–5, 229
lifecycle, 128
Limits to Growth, The, 48
Lovelock, James, 2
'Lucas critique', 52

Macmillan, Harold, 42
'Magnificent Seven' tech
    companies, 96, 177
mainstream economics, 27–9,
    33
Malthus, Thomas Robert, 48
Marshall, George, 41
Marshall Plan, 41
Marx, Karl, 28, 120, 197–8,
    200, 202, 236
McKinsey & Co., 6, 216
'Me and Bobby McGee'
    (song), 134–5
medicine, 187–9
mental health, 189–93
Meta, 96

Mexico, 78, 136–7
Microsoft, 96
Milanovic, Branko, 28
Mill, John Stuart, 28, 199, 236
Minsky, Hyman, 92
Mitchell, Joni, 47
mobile technology, 213–14
Modern Monetary Theory, 117
monetary theory, 52
Music Room, The (film), 119–20

NASDAQ Clean Edge Green Energy Index, 220
National debt, 142
nature, 19–21, 32, 38, 46–9
  man's relationship with, 3–5, 19–21, 24–5, 31, 35
  mythology and, 20–22
neoclassical school of economics, 7, 60, 141, 190, 194–5, 197–200
Netherlands, 43
Nietzsche, Friedrich, 199, 200, 202
Niger, 100–101
Nigeria, 65
NIMBYism, 129, 131
Nordhaus, William, 60–61
North Macedonia, 79
Norway, 117
Nvidia, 96

Ohmae, Kenichi, 89
oil crisis (1973), 48–9

'old friends' theory, 188
Organisation for Economic Co-operation and Development (OECD), 126
Ottawa, Canada, 54–5
Oxford Economics, 137

Pakistan, 212
Paris Agreement (2015), 148
Parrique, Timothée, 27
pension funds, 125–6, 218–20, 233–5
Peru, 78
Philippines, 101
Phoenix, Arizona, 166
Pigou, Arthur, 29
'political economy', 195
pollution, 57, 59, 61
population
  age, 12, 103–5
  falling population, 144
  global population, 44, 48
populism, 144, 172, 234
Portugal, 43, 78, 151
post-development thought, 52–3
poverty, 60, 153, 190
productivity, 4, 17, 104–7, 112, 135–40, 166, 171, 177–84

rail infrastructure, 166
Rand, Tom, 218, 225
Raworth, Kate, 27
Ray, Satyajit, 119

real estate, 128–31, 154, 162, 164–6, 221
  bubbles, 121
  climate change and, 162, 164–7, 169, 171–2
  insurance, 165
Reeves, Rachel, 232
religion, 20–22, 36
renewable energy, 208–26
  economic renewal and, 223–6
  investment in, 216–24
rentier economy, 143
retirement, 105, 125
Ricardo, David, 28
Rio Earth Summit (1992), 52–4
Rise and Fall of American Growth, The (Gordon), 182
risk management
  anticipation, 90–91
  resilience, 90–91
risk-taking, 134–5
'Roaring Twenties', 6–7, 9, 74–5, 93, 95, 102–5
Robinson, James, 112, 201
Rodrik, Dani, 112
Roman Empire, 111
Romanticism, 26, 46–7
Romer, Paul, 113
Roux, Joubert, 210–11, 213, 215–16
Russia, 34
Rwanda, 100
  Rwandan genocide (1994), 66

Sachs, Wolfgang, 53
Sahm, Claudia, 191
SARS, 67, 68
savings rates, 126
Scandinavia, 62
Schumacher, E.F., 51–2
Schumpeter, Joseph, 120–21, 200–202
science, 22–6, 28–9, 36–7
scientific revolution, 204–5
Searching for Safety (Wildavsky), 90
Second World War (1939–45), 40, 44, 118
  postwar Britain, 40
  postwar Germany, 40–41
  postwar USA, 40–42
Serbia, 79
shipping industry 89–90
Sierra Leone, 212
Silver, Nick, 217
Singapore, 65, 217
Singh, Manmohan, 110
slavery, 36
Small Is Beautiful (Schumacher), 51
Smith, Adam, 28, 196, 236
Smith, Noah, 175
social media, 106, 177–8, 181, 183
societal resilience, 88–93
solar energy, 212, 215, 217, 224
Solar Panda, 214, 215, 218
Solow, Robert, 112, 179, 184
Solow-Swan model, 112, 142

South Africa, 69–70, 76, 78, 138, 210–12, 217
South Korea, 65
South Sudan, 72, 79
Soviet Union, 139, 188
Spain, 226
Spengler, Oswald, 199
Starmer, Keir, 231
Steinbeck, John, 130
structuralism, 30
Sudan, 100
supply chains, 89–90
Swan, Trevor, 112
Switzerland, 62

Taleb, Nassim Nicholas, 159–60
technological innovation, 106–7, 112–13, 119–21, 134–6, 177–85
telegraph, 182–3
Tesla, 96
'Tragedy of the Commons, The' (Hardin), 47
Trump, Donald, 34, 87, 98–9, 142, 215, 221, 232
Truss, Liz, 231

Ukraine, 34
United Kingdom, 43, 78, 138, 142, 176, 204–5
 climate change and, 172
 Covid-19 and, 88, 95–6, 159–60
 economic growth rate, 204–5
 life expectancy, 125
 national debt, 116
 pensions, 126
 postwar, 40–41
 wealth, 143, 233
United States, 8, 78, 96–8, 138
 American exceptionalism, 8, 96–7
 Big Beautiful Bill (2025), 142, 176
 climate change and, 165–6
 Congressional Budget Office, 97
 Covid-19 and, 87–8, 95–7
 dollar, 97, 99
 'golden age' (1948–73), 41–3, 96–7
 Great Depression, 130, 201
 Immigration and Customs Enforcement (ICE), 145
 labour productivity, 178–9, 181–2
 national debt, 97–8, 115
 population age, 103
 postwar, 40–42
 renewable energy and, 215
 savings rate, 126
 tariffs, 98
 technological innovation, 135, 177–9
 wealth in, 233
University of Notre Dame, Indiana, 62
US National Institutes of Health, 158

V-Dem project, 230
Vietnam, 100

wealth, 11–13, 107–8, 114, 122, 139–43, 154, 233
   population ageing and, 124–9
   wealth trap, 123–4, 228
welfare state, 30
Western world, 3, 7, 12, 30, 35–6, 68, 102–3
   climate change and, 62, 150–51, 172–3
   Covid-19 and, 68–9, 71–3, 79
   labour productivity, 105–6
   life expectancy, 105–6
   national debt, 116–19, 142
   population age, 103–5
   see also economic growth, 180
Why Empires Fall (Rapley & Heather), 8
Why Nations Fail (Acemoglu & Robinson), 112, 201–2
Wilberforce, Samuel, 22
Wildavsky, Aaron, 90
Wilson, Harold, 204–5
World Happiness Report, 191

zoonotic diseases, 9, 67, 81, 146, 158–9, 161–2
Zoroastrianism, 21

A Note on the Author

John Rapley is an author and academic who divides his time among London, Johannesburg and Ottawa. His books include *Twilight of the Money Gods* and *Why Empires Fall* (co-authored with Peter Heather).